"Life is often difficult and sometimes painful. This pain can either push us away from God or draw us closer to Him. In *Don't Waste the Pain*, David Lyons and his sister Linda Richardson blend Scripture and their own experiences with cancer to teach us how pain can draw us closer to God. But this is more than a book about fighting cancer; it is a book about God and pain. And because we all experience pain—be it physical, emotional, or spiritual—from time to time, every believer can profit from this book."

—JERRY BRIDGES, author of *Respectable Sins*,
The Pursuit of Holiness, and *Trusting God*

"Eloquently written, profoundly helpful, deeply thoughtful, engagingly funny, and heart-wrenchingly real—this is an amazing book! Walking with David and Renee through these years of pain has been one of the great privileges of my life. Reading this book has clarified important lessons for me. I hope I do not recover!"

—MIKE TRENEER, international president, The Navigators

"I couldn't put this book down. It is loaded with priceless insights into the deepest questions we all have about pain, suffering, and God and His ways. The authors—David Lyons and his sister Linda Richardson—write in real time. They take the reader with them as they process good news and bad, as she grapples with her cancer and he with his son Ian's illness and eventual death. We get in on their journal notes and exchanges of correspondence. Because of what they could see from where they were standing at the time, their observations repeatedly offer new understandings of Scripture and of God Himself. Surprisingly, this book is upbeat and filled with joy."

—JIM PETERSEN, author of *Living Proof, Lifestyle Discipleship*,
and *Church Without Walls*

DON'T WASTE the PAIN

LEARNING TO GROW THROUGH SUFFERING

DAVID LYONS *and*
LINDA LYONS RICHARDSON

NAVPRESS

Discipleship Inside Out™

Discipleship Inside Out™

NavPress is the publishing ministry of The Navigators, an international Christian organization and leader in personal spiritual development. NavPress is committed to helping people grow spiritually and enjoy lives of meaning and hope through personal and group resources that are biblically rooted, culturally relevant, and highly practical.

For a free catalog go to www.NavPress.com
or call 1.800.366.7788 in the United States or 1.800.839.4769 in Canada.

NAVPRESS and the NAVPRESS logo are registered trademarks of NavPress. Absence of ® in connection with marks of NavPress or other parties does not indicate an absence of registration of those marks.

ISBN-13: 978-1-61521-548-5

Cover design by Arvid Wallen
Cover photography by David Lyons
Interior photography by Steve Richardson, David Lyons, and Werner Pieper

Some of the anecdotal illustrations in this book are true to life and are included with the permission of the persons involved. All other illustrations are composites of real situations, and any resemblance to people living or dead is coincidental.

Scripture versions used include: the *Holy Bible, New International Version®* (NIV®). Copyright © 1973, 1978, 1984 by International Bible Society. Used by permission of Zondervan. All rights reserved; the New American Standard Bible (NASB), Copyright © 1960, 1962, 1963, 1968, 1971, 1972, 1973, 1975, 1977, 1995 by The Lockman Foundation. Used by permission; the New King James Version (NKJV). Copyright © 1982 by Thomas Nelson, Inc. Used by permission. All rights reserved; *THE MESSAGE* (MSG). Copyright © 1993, 1994, 1995, 1996, 2000, 2001, 2002. Used by permission of NavPress Publishing Group; and the *Holy Bible*, New Living Translation (NLT), copyright © 1996, 2004. Used by permission of Tyndale House Publishers, Inc., Wheaton, Illinois 60189. All rights reserved; *The New Testament in Modern English* (PH), J. B. Phillips Translator, © J. B. Phillips 1958, 1960, 1972, used by permission of Macmillan Publishing Company; and the King James Version (KJV).

Library of Congress Cataloging-in-Publication Data

Lyons, David, 1955-
  Don't waste the pain : learning to grow through suffering / David Lyons and Linda Lyons Richardson.
    p. cm.
  Includes bibliographical references.
  ISBN 978-1-61521-548-5
  1. Suffering--Religious aspects--Christianity. 2. Cancer--Religious aspects--Christianity. I. Richardson, Linda Lyons. II. Title.
  BV4909.L96 2010
  248.8'6--dc22
                          2010004812

Printed in the United States of America

1 2 3 4 5 6 7 8 / 14 13 12 11 10

To Ian and those who loved him

CONTENTS

FOREWORD

By Dr. Larry Crabb

Do not expect my foreword to offer either a critique of this book or an easily marketed endorsement. I was far too personally caught up in what I read on every page to respond from an evaluative distance or to cheerily advertise its message. The two authors, brother and sister David and Linda, wouldn't let me hide from the fear that I know is rumbling somewhere inside me, the fear that I prefer to leave buried beneath promises God hasn't made.

Worse, they stripped away whatever remnants remain of naive "Christian" optimism and fluffy "biblical" theology that tell me to believe God will somehow numb the pain of whatever suffering He calls me to endure. After reading only a few pages, I put the book down, looked nowhere in particular, and, with a freshness I didn't much like, acknowledged what I'd rather deny: *I'm scared and pain hurts.* God offers no guarantee that what I dread will never happen, not to me; and He makes no promise to provide anesthesia if it does.

When I wrote the book titled *Shattered Dreams,* one publisher decided not to print it. No one, they told me, would read a book with such a negative message. I predict and I fervently pray that many, hopefully hundreds of thousands, will read *Don't Waste the Pain.* Its message is not only *not* negative, it is as laced with hope as spring after a long, hard winter.

David and Linda make the outrageous claim — no, they live the unpopular truth — that life-giving hope grows in the raw realism of suffering. In undiluted pain, the God who is there becomes slowly recognized as the God who is here. And joy erupts in the unlikeliest moments. Laughter, too. I remember my father saying as we drove to the cemetery to bury my brother who had just died in a plane crash, "No one would think to tell us a joke today. I wish they would. It would help me know there is always cause for joy."

Of course, tears continue to flow. Hearts still ache, at times with searing agony that makes laughter impossible. But somehow life happens, real life, eternal life; it springs up through the snow. As Emily Dickinson expressed it, truth that we've long believed but never really knew becomes a vision that "dazzles gradually." In darkness we strangely become more alive than we were in daylight.

Halfway through this book, I heard myself saying what King Agrippa said to Paul: "A little more, and your arguments would make me a Christian" (see Acts 26:28). Then I read a little more, and three truths became slowly dazzling.

First, *deep faith develops in authentic community.* Legendary psychologist O. Hobart Mowrer remained an atheist in part because, as he once told John Stott, "The church has not learned the secret of community." If the secret is authenticity that draws us to God — and I believe it is — then *Don't Waste the Pain* reveals that secret to the church.

Second, *living in the moment of our story lifts us into the passion of God's story.* The unseen and too often unfelt drama of God's good plan becomes more visible and real, more dazzling, when life in this world leaves us only two choices: despair in misery or dependence on God.

Third, *the much-needed shift from routine belief to resolute conviction happens when we hear truth that's lived by people we trust.* Paul told Timothy to "remain faithful to the things you have been taught. You know they are true, for you know you can trust those who taught you"

(2 Timothy 3:14, NLT). David and his wife buried their thirteen-year-old son after a two-year battle against a rare form of cancer, after thousands of prayers for his healing. Linda writes during a ten-year and still continuing battle with cancer.

I survived cancer thirteen years ago. I was given a clean bill of health. Until a few months ago, when a yearly test revealed that the cancer is back. Mine is a slow-growing form that doesn't usually metastasize. I might die from natural causes after a long and healthy-feeling life. That's possible, even likely.

But like you, and like David and Linda, I have no promise from God that I will live another year. And I have no provision from God that will numb whatever suffering lies ahead. But like you, and like David and Linda, I do have both promise and provision from God that when I go through deep waters I will not drown, that I am precious to God, that I am empowered to reveal His glory and to become more like His Son in any circumstance.

The uniquely candid and current journey we've been invited to join in this book will help convince you, as it has me, that deep faith grows in authentic community, that embracing where we are in our story releases us to live in the joy and hope of His story, and that those who walk ahead of us on the narrow road to life can give us courage to follow, to not waste our pain, to learn what it means to grow through suffering. God is *always* doing us good, even in the worst of times, when all the lights go out. Dawn will come. We will not only survive. We will *live*.

ACKNOWLEDGMENTS

From David:

This book is essentially a chapter from my life and walk with God, so there are countless people who have shaped me and therefore shaped the book. I will not begin to name the friends who have deeply influenced how I see the role of pain in spiritual formation. But I do want to offer a group hug to my Navigator family, a worldwide network of friends and co-workers who have loved me and inspired me for many years. Your fingerprints are on my life and on this book.

There are countless people who have carried us through our most difficult days. But I am most grateful to those in our International Office who have walked with me through the most difficult five years of my life, and thus have often carried an extra load for their wounded brother. Most recently they graciously gave me six weeks of leave to begin recovering from my son's suffering and death and to finish writing this book. Without that time and space, a great idea would have become a destructive burden.

Most of all, I am grateful for my family. This is *our* story. I am among those who stand in awe of my wife, Renee, who has suffered so much and stands so tall through it all. Many feared that our children would be crushed by our pain. Instead, each of them has become more rather than less through what we have suffered. I am incredibly proud of each one. Renee's siblings and my siblings (including Linda) have demonstrated what it means to sacrificially *be there* for those you love. We have the privilege of enjoying siblings whom we would choose as our friends.

From Linda:

The physical and emotional pain of the past nine years has been tremendous, but not just for me. More than once my husband and children have had to consider life without me. My sister, Marilyn, and brother, David, and both of their families joined us from day one in prayer and support. When Ian was diagnosed, we all added him to our ongoing prayers. I thank God for blessing each of us with a clearer understanding of who He is while I (we) lived through it. That has made my own pain worth enduring.

I look back to the 1950s when our family had but one believer, our mom. Over time, our dad and each child and grandchild she loved came to know Christ. Ian was the first to join his grandparents, but we'll all be together again.

Thank you to Pastor Gordon Cathey (retired, Christian Missionary Alliance) for leading me to faith in Christ, and Pastor John Winterstein (Salem Evangelical Church of New Holland, Pennsylvania) for the truth and insight you graciously taught me over the years. Because of your teaching, I know Him. Thank you to Charles Boice, MD, my oncologist. Your ongoing wisdom and gentle kindness have extended and blessed my life. Thank you to my Calvert County Bible study and Grace Evangelical Church. Your ongoing prayers, comfort, and meals have seen me through many difficult times. Thank you to my coauthor and brother, David Lyons. You are my dear friend and faithful encourager. Thank you to my daughter, Morgan, and son, Sam. You give me a reason to keep going and make me laugh through it all. And finally, thank you to my husband, Steve. Your laughter, love, encouragement, and belief in me continually make my life worth living.

From Both of Us:

Finally, we need to say that in our editor, Leura Jones, God has given us a rare gift. Leura and her family walked with David's family through the valley of the shadow of death, so she approached this project with more than professional interest. As a result, we found it easy to trust her with editing our most intimate and passionate thoughts. She poured into this book not only her skills but also her heart. Without her touch, this book would lack the gourmet seasoning that you will now enjoy.

How Our
Story Began

Flashing lights on the horizon told us that someone's life had probably been changed forever. Grim policemen hurried us by. Like the other rubberneckers, we slowed down and peered over to see the wreckage. *What is it that compels us to look at someone else's pain?*

My sister Linda and I (David) give you permission to peer into the "collisions" that have consumed our lives. It's okay. Don't rush by. You can take a closer look. If you don't, you might miss the treasure hidden there.

Cancer broke into each of our homes like a burly invader breaking down the back door. Linda's invasion came in September 2000 when she was diagnosed with stage-IIIC clear-cell ovarian cancer and rushed into surgery. Ours came in February 2008 when our twelve-year-old son Ian was diagnosed with stage-IV alveolar rhabdomyosarcoma, a very rare cancer that kills 98 percent of its victims.

Most of us live life assuming that the really bad stuff only happens to other people. We naively think, *It will never happen to me!* But pain broke into our lives and took over. It became a daily companion. Fear and anger crept in, too. As we lived through it, Linda and I both processed through writing. It's like therapy for us, digesting truth and confirming it in our hearts as we write. A CaringBridge website made it easy for friends to follow our story. Ian's story went viral on the Internet, and within weeks of his diagnosis, thousands of people were praying with us. Six months later, people on six continents were celebrating the report that Ian was cancer free.

So in October 2008, Linda and I were able to catch our breath and begin shaping our story into this book. Then the invader broke down the back door again. By January 2009 Linda's cancer had come back for the fourth time, and Ian began showing symptoms of brain trauma. The cancer had gone into hiding and crossed the blood-brain barrier, taking refuge in his brain and growing there aggressively.

That launched us into another odyssey. Along with many others, we were deeply convinced that God would heal Ian again. Confirmation came through a brain scan in April, when our neurologist told us it looked like the cancer in Ian's brain was being defeated even though the chemo was not working. But the very next day it manifested in his lungs. Our warrior boy was rushed to the hospital for a final battle and was welcomed into heaven the following Monday.

Our beliefs have been tested and matured through our pain. We did not set out to develop a theology of suffering or healing. You will not find that here. We have just tried to walk with God as we know Him, then share that with you. The best definition of *discipleship* that I know is "letting someone else in on your walk with God." We have lived out this drama with friends from varied streams of the Christian faith: Baptist and Charismatic, Orthodox and Episcopalian, Catholic and Presbyterian. We embrace the fact that readers of this book will have very different views on the sovereignty of God, the responsibility of man, the ultimate origins of suffering and pain, and our roles and responsibilities in healing. So as you read, we urge you to simply chew up the meat, spit out the bones, and allow us to be our authentic selves with you.

I'm writing this preface only a few weeks after Ian's death. Linda is writing in the midst of her ten-year battle with cancer. Most of this book was written "live," right from the midst of whatever we were facing. You won't be reading our memories; you'll be journeying with us, and we welcome you as guests, not voyeurs.

Soon after his daughter was diagnosed with leukemia, Pastor John Claypool's friend asked, "Those of us who have not been there wonder what it is like in the Darkness. Can you tell us?" We're writing from smack-dab in the middle of our darkness—and our moments of great joy—so that you can grow with us. Be prepared to laugh, too. Sometimes laughing is the only thing that helps.

It's very likely you are reading this book because pain has broken into your house. We hope you're here because you want to grow through what you're facing. You want to become better rather than bitter. You want to be full again, not empty. Believe it or not, you can be.

We hope that reading this book will inspire you to take further steps to grow through whatever pain may come your way. As you read, you can come to *dontwastethepain.com* and build on what you are learning here.

Join a discussion of others' stories of how they are growing through many kinds of pain. Digest life-changing truths. Join a virtual small group led by a mentor. Or join as a family, a Sunday school class, or a small group that wants to learn to grow together.

J. B. Phillips translated James 1:2-5 this way:

When all kinds of trials and temptations crowd into your lives, my brothers, don't resent them as intruders, but welcome them as friends! Realise that they come to test your faith and to produce in you the quality of endurance. But let the process go on until that endurance is fully developed, and you will find you have become men of mature character, men of integrity with no weak spots. And if, in the process, any of you does not know how to meet any particular problem he has only to ask God—who gives generously to all men without making them feel guilty—and he may be quite sure that the necessary wisdom will be given him.

You may not be quite ready to welcome your intruder as a friend. But if you'd like to grow through it, if you'd like to know how one would possibly say, "I wouldn't wish the pain away for anything," then you're reading the right book. May you find in these pages the wisdom promised by James to those who seek it. We suggest that you pause and ask God for that wisdom before you begin.

David Lyons and Linda Lyons Richardson
June 4, 2009

CHAPTER 1

WELCOME TO OZ

H ave you ever felt like you've woken up in some strange land where nothing seems right or familiar? Like you're Dorothy in the middle of Oz, wondering how in the world you got there?

I (David) often felt like that on the first day of school. I'd gotten comfortable in my old classroom. The unknown future looked like the dark and mysterious woods in Oz. But I don't remember ever being given the opportunity to stay back (although I imagine some of my teachers seriously considered holding me back!). Instead, I was pushed along into the next maze of new classes and challenges.

Likewise, Linda and I don't recall signing up for the challenges cancer brought our way. Maybe at one time or another we naively prayed some audacious prayers, asking God to do "whatever it takes" to make us more like Him. We didn't think He would take us so seriously. But He took our prayers at face value and went to work as a chiropractor determined to straighten us out, even if it required some painful adjustments that knocked the breath out of us.

God was preparing us for a new way of Life, a journey that took us many miles through the valley of tears. Here's a glimpse of how my sister Linda had descended into that valley:

I WISH I WAS DEAD

September 2000

Linda before cancer

"I wish I was dead." That was my response when my husband, Steve, asked me one night why I was crying. He'd brushed his hand over my cheek after we went to bed, and he felt my tears in the darkness. I'd been quietly crying, hoping he wouldn't notice. I was crying because I hated my life.

For two years, I'd made one lousy decision after another. Devastation from a lost job, broken friendships, and family problems had led me toward clinical depression, barely able to function. Not trusting anyone to work with me, I started my own pottery shop. An acquaintance came by to look at it and said, "I bet you'll love this place; you must be excited about it." "It's okay," I said, still wary and hurting from my losses, "but frankly, I don't care if it burns to the ground. I'll never love a job again. It's not worth the pain if you lose it."

A few days later, my first shipment of pots arrived; I set them up, moving them from an outer wall to an inner wall. The next day, I received a call from one of the landlords while I was working on setting up my insurance coverage. He told me that during the night our building had burned to the ground, a total loss. My pots weren't burned, but the previous day I'd restacked them at what turned out to be the source of the fire, so the firemen had to throw them out of the way, shattering all but a few. The outer area was untouched.

Was God mocking me? Had He heard me say I didn't care? I picked myself up and started again at a new location, only to have the new landlord dispute my inventory and sell it for himself, never paying me for most of it. Crushed once again, I managed to move to yet another "fabulous" location.

While this was going on, our mom had developed vascular dementia, and our dad had leg surgery that didn't go well. I had to miss my son's first day of school to go to the hospital, and on and on it went. It was like being slapped in the face day after day. Putting one foot in front of the other took all I had.

Eventually, I just wished I was dead. All I wanted to do was go to sleep and not wake up. I hated every minute of every day, and there was nothing Steve could do for me. God couldn't either, as far as I was concerned. Of course, I wasn't exactly putting Him at the forefront of my life, so how would I know what He could do?

So, I wished I was dead. And I meant it.

REAL FUNNY, GOD!

Just a few weeks later, Linda found out that she might get her wish.

Cancer seemed like a cruel joke that caught me completely by surprise. Other people get cancer; I don't. My initial symptoms were so harmless that I didn't even consider seeking treatment. I wasn't hungry. "Uh-oh! Call an ambulance! I'm not hungry!" I had a stomachache every so often and gas pains once in a while. Now which of those would send anyone to the doctor? There was bloating, but I also got quite thin. I wasn't big to begin with, and I was doing a lot of physical work, which I assumed led to the weight loss. No two things were ever evident at the same time either; it was just every so often.

Then it started to feel as though I was sitting on the business end of a baseball bat when I sat down. Now that was disconcerting. Eventually, I started to notice the uncomfortable symptoms more frequently. Steve began to notice that I complained more often that I didn't feel well. We assumed I wasn't eating right, or was stressed, or was too busy at my job. Then my lower abdomen started to look swollen. I was skin and bone with a little swelling on one side of my belly. Now that was weird.

Finally, I cried out in pain one day during sexual intercourse with my husband. "That's it," he said. "You're going to a doctor." I went to see my doc and told her of my embarrassingly mild, stupid symptoms. I apologized for wasting her time on such an insignificant thing. I probably just had indigestion.

She had me lie down on the gurney and lightly touched my abdomen. The excruciating pain almost threw me onto the floor. Eyes wide open, I looked at her in horror. Looking almost as stunned as I felt, she said quietly, "I think you need to see a specialist." I went in for a CT scan, a transnational sonogram, a colonoscopy, and blood tests, among other things. Two doctors confirmed that I had an ovarian cyst, and surgery was scheduled for the following week. Easy enough—though surgery, however minor, is never convenient.

When I went in a few days later for pre-op testing and preparation, my OB/GYN came back into the room just before I was ready to leave. We talked for a few minutes, and then in the sweetest and gentlest way I could imagine, she said, "We did a blood test on you as a matter of routine with cases like yours. Linda, it's not a cyst. You have ovarian cancer."

I remember smiling, silently thinking, *No, I don't. I don't get cancer. But you're so sweet to be so nice about it.* All I got out was an incredulous "Really?"

She told me that a blood test (called a CA-125) of 30 or less was in the normal range. Hormones could affect the readings. If a test revealed anything over 30, cancer would be considered. Over 100 would require immediate treatment. (Just as a point of reference, in the ensuing years, I've never personally met anyone with a reading of more than 250, which is usually considered stage IV.)

Mine was 13,000. No typo, three zeros.

I didn't stand a chance.

"Real funny, God. I didn't think You'd take me seriously!" I'd really meant it three weeks earlier when I said I wished I was dead—at least I thought I did. Yeah, I really did. I hated my life, didn't I? Was the God I thought I knew, yet rarely listened to, really listening to me? Was this His answer?

That night, a mere month after the tears, I lay next to Steve, wondering what to say. I reminded him of the day I'd told him we were pregnant for the first time. Back then, unable to think of a clever way to tell him the news, I'd just blurted it out. This time I said, "Remember when I told you I was pregnant with Morgan? Well, I can't think of a clever way to tell you this either, but I have cancer." There was a long sigh as all the air flowed out of his lungs. We talked for a few minutes, and then I fell asleep; he left to walk the darkened peninsula alone for a long time.

And so my journey began. But I wouldn't be alone.

EVERYONE'S WORST NIGHTMARE

Linda and I had not been particularly close as children, and that gap widened when I started following Christ. I'll never forget her response when I wrote a letter to my big sister telling her that I'd opened my heart to Christ. She wrote back, "I used to think that you had a brain." I still have that letter in my desk. Years later, my wife, Renee, and I moved to Washington, D.C., where Linda and Steve lived, and she said to Renee with a mixture of astonishment and disgust, "All our friends are *Christians*." God had surrounded them in answer to our prayers, and soon they too were born of the Spirit. Although that was decades ago, I've never gotten over the wonder of seeing Linda follow Christ. She's called herself my pagan big sister. But we've grown close, and cancer broke down any walls that may have remained. We walked the cancer road with Linda for several years. We helped run her business when she was too sick. We sat by her bed not knowing what to say. We learned the value of saying nothing and just being there. Then, in 2004, God moved my family 1,600 miles across the country, from Virginia to Colorado. There He introduced us to pain of our very own. It was like nothing we'd ever known.

One day a couple of years into our own saga, I forced myself to put one foot in front of the other as I walked from my office to the men's room. I must have looked drunk. I wasn't. I wasn't even physically tired. But I was emotionally spent. A phone call from Renee had confronted me with another family crisis crashing down on us. It seemed I had been getting calls like this nearly every month, like waves pounding against the rocks one after another.

Before moving to Colorado, we had lived a charmed life. Our ministry had flourished. God had blessed us with seven beautiful children. The week we left Virginia a hundred of our closest friends gathered to honor us and send us off. Many had a larger-than-life view of us. We were moving because I had been honored with a big promotion, and it seemed like we were moving to the Promised Land.

Instead, the stress of the move boiled issues to the surface one after another. Soon two children manifested serious eating disorders. A month later, I received an urgent call from a friend in Virginia telling me that one of my children was attempting suicide as we spoke. Later that summer, I was called out of leader meetings to learn that three of my children had been molested by someone in the neighborhood.

It didn't end there. That fall a counselor called us into his office so one of our children could tell us of sexual abuse by a family member years before. Then one of our teens began careening toward self-destruction, getting into trouble with the law and asserting he had gotten a girl pregnant and would be leaving school to support her.

Promised Land, huh?

At the same time, my promotion was leading me into a buzz saw of rejection and frustration at work. And dreams of planting a simple church in our home went up in smoke as we focused on merely surviving.

Then my wife began having flashbacks of horrific things she had experienced as a child. I had often referred to Renee as Wonder Woman and our children as the Seven Wonders of the World. But Wonder Woman was coming apart at the seams.

My life was coming apart at the seams.

Three years into all of this, it seemed like the worst might be over. Then our sixth child, twelve-year-old Ian, began experiencing chronic cold and flu symptoms and back pain. With so many children, we've been around the block a few times with childhood illnesses. We don't get alarmed easily. But one Saturday night we noticed a bruise on Ian's foot was growing rather than healing. We made plans to take him in for an exam Monday morning. We never made it to that appointment.

The next night Ian developed searing back pain. We took him to the ER in the middle of the night. Before noon, a doctor pulled Renee and me into a conference room. I don't remember all that she said. After the words *stage-IV cancer*, the room went gray. She left us to sob until we could sob no more and to gather ourselves so we could tell Ian.

In the coming days we learned that the cancer had destroyed 95 percent of Ian's bone marrow and that a tumor filling his abdomen was doubling in size every forty-eight hours. No wonder his back hurt.

The pain filling Ian's body was filling my own heart.

Ian before cancer

TWO PHONE CALLS

February 4, 2008
The Day Ian Was Diagnosed

Dave's call knocked the breath out of me. I thought, *This can't be happening to my brother's son. Think fast. He needs you to be strong and wise right now. Say the right thing: "Okay, what's next? Do you need me out there? I'll fly out whenever you want."* It was surreal to talk about this horrible thing. Over the past seven and a half years, my cancer had become a part of my own fabric, but this? My twelve-year-old nephew? It was mind numbing.

I hung up the phone and sat down. Minutes passed. I knew I should call Steve. I felt unable to move. The phone rang again.

"Hi, it's Hollis." Even while in remission, I still had monthly blood tests, and Hollis always called with my CA-125 results. "I'm afraid it's back, Linda. Your numbers have climbed into a bad range again. You'll probably have to go back into chemo, but you need to see Dr. Boice soon."

I sat there looking out the window. It felt dreamlike, unreal—yet this was very real. Two phone calls had changed my entire world. I actually felt a rush of adrenaline, knowing that what lay before our family was something most people would never have to experience. I was angry, exhausted, sad, even exhilarated, but never afraid.

I knew that David and his whole family were about to enter into the world where Steve and I had lived so long: the life of living with cancer. After my initial plunge into this whole cancer life—when the hair was gone, the body scarred and forever changed, the outcome uncertain, our life an entire paradigm shift—Steve told me one day, "Honey, we're not in Kansas anymore." Nothing was the same, nothing was normal, nothing could be predicted. The surreal had become the norm. We were in Oz, and now David had to live there too. I knew I'd be there with him, for him.

I recalled an e-mail he'd sent me a few years earlier, after I'd been living in Oz for a while:

Dear Linda,
Whenever I think of you and pray for you these days, I
feel this strange mixture of sadness, hope, wonder, and joy.
The sadness is, of course, about the pain and discomfort
of your body and the "inconvenience" of your circumstances.
The hope, wonder, and joy are over the beauty of your
spirit, your inner person that God has so transformed.
You amaze me. And you bring tears to my eyes.
Love,
Your little brother

I had to call Steve, tell him about Ian, tell him my own cancer was back. And while I was at it, perhaps I should finally tell him that my mammogram the previous week showed a suspicious spot and I was scheduled for a sonogram in three weeks. Oh, and my doctor told me to have an abnormal mole examined because it looked suspiciously like melanoma. I should tell him I have to see a dermatologist about that. I couldn't protect him from any of this any longer.

Or maybe I could just go to sleep and never wake up.

EPISTLES FROM AN INTENSIVE CARE UNIT

From David's Journal
February 4, 2008

I will always remember February 4 as one of the most difficult days of my life — the day that we learned Ian has cancer. I don't think I've ever cried so much in one day or even in a week. I feel numb. At the same time, I have strong confidence in God's loving care and sovereign control. I wouldn't say that I'm worried. Each day has enough trouble of its own. I'm just putting one foot in front of the other.

My prayers are minimal — just breath-prayers for the most part, sighs toward God. I know that He's hovering here, watching over us, especially watching over Ian. I imagine that there are angels stationed at the door of the ICU and even in this room.

Friends have been wonderful. We are bathed in love and offers of help. Of course, what we want most is beyond their human reach. Yet is healing what we want most? I doubt it. More than anything I want Ian to know You deeply, and I pray that through this you two will become intimate friends. Help him learn to pour out his heart to You. Help me lead him in this by example. I've prayed regularly that Ian would come to know Your love through me. May it be so even now.

But I also pray for miraculous healing. I've experienced that myself in my own body. I've seen it again and again in my sister. Nothing is too difficult for You. It is a matter of asking and trusting. I do trust You, Lord. I've learned that trusting You does not mean that You will never hurt us. But I trust You anyway, with full confidence that You are truly working for our good.

February 5, 2008

We've just finished the second day of this — this what? Adventure? Ordeal? Test? It's all of that. It's been so intense. I've not left the hospital since early yesterday morning, nearly *forty-eight* hours now. Today I did not have a chance to eat breakfast until 3:30 p.m. Now it's nearly 11 p.m., and I'm sitting in a dark room preparing for another night with Ian. It is finally quiet. How can my heart be in such pain and yet so much at peace? Peace prevails, and I long for Ian to experience that too. He seems to be receiving some of that. Mostly he's just getting through the pain and discomfort, and beginning to take it all in to the degree he can at *twelve* years old. I imagine that in many ways this will shape his passage into manhood. He is showing great courage and composure and resolve. In the midst of tough days ahead, may he come to know You deeply. And may he come to know Your love through me.

February 7, 2008

Harsh realities continue. Tonight we received the definite diagnosis. Now we are bracing ourselves for twelve months of treatment, including chemotherapy, radiation therapy, and a bone marrow transplant. We also plan to support that with nutritional therapy.

For years before this ICU encounter, I'd been preaching my life message, "Live Jesus," from 2 Corinthians 4:7-11:

> But we have this treasure in jars of clay to show that this all-surpassing power is from God and not from us. We are hard pressed on every side, but not crushed; perplexed, but not in despair; persecuted, but not abandoned; struck down, but not destroyed. We always carry around in our body the death of Jesus, so that the life of Jesus may also be revealed in our body. For we who are alive are always being given over to death for Jesus' sake, so that his life may be revealed in our mortal body. (NIV)

Often as I shared from this passage, I'd think to myself, *But our life has been relatively easy. I think there may be much harder things coming down the road for us.* I was right.

So Linda and I found ourselves settling into Oz. And as Dorothy discovered, Oz can be a frightening place. But as surreal as our arrival was, this place has been more real than any place we've ever lived.

Now that you've stepped into our story, you can close this book and pretend you live in a world without pain. You can hope it never happens to you. Or you can follow us down the yellow brick road to

Life as it was always designed to be lived. You see, the world we live in is a broken place, a shadow of life as it was supposed to be and as it will someday be in heaven. There, where my son lives, there is no pain. But here on earth, pain is our companion. We can deny it. We can fight it. Or we can receive it as a gift.

QUESTIONS FOR REFLECTION

- ▶ What does *your* "Oz" look like?
- ▶ In what ways do you identify with David and Linda?
- ▶ What do you hope to get out of reading this book?

CHAPTER 2

PAIN: THE GIFT NOBODY WANTS

When I got home, I opened the trunk and saw it: a dead raccoon. For several years this flea-bitten carcass had been passed from colleague to colleague as a joke during our annual staff retreat. One day long ago someone had paid a taxidermist to preserve the poor fellow. He must have had bad karma to be condemned to being tossed from one garage to another, despised by every owner who inherited him. Each year it became more difficult to trick others into taking him home. This year he was ours, the gift nobody wanted.

Pain can be like that. We admire others who endure it well. From a distance they look so noble, and sometimes we can even see how God has used it for their good. That's fine until it lands on your porch, in your family, in your body. But unlike that poor raccoon, pain really is a precious gift. There is hidden treasure reserved for those who find and follow God's path in and through the pain. But it's not always pretty.

GOD, PLEASE MAKE IT STOP

From Linda's Journal
October 2000

The pain is almost more than I can bear. All I want is to be naked and float in the air with nothing touching me anywhere. It hurts to sit, lie down, stand, walk, eat, breathe, sleep. It hurts to be alive. The pain is unceasing. Is there no end? God, please make it stop.

It feels as though half of my insides are gone, cut out to save my life. I can feel my body parts not being there. It all hurts: the cut and stapled skin, the inside of my body—(Excuse me, have you ever felt the inside of your own body? Are you even aware of it? I don't mean a tummyache; I mean have you ever felt your own colon? I think we feel our own body only when it hurts, and I am acutely aware of my entire body.)—the bone and muscular soreness, the weariness, not to mention the horrid effects of the chemo. I throw up, I can't eat, I can barely walk, and every inch of me hurts. Every strand of hair hurts. My teeth hurt. Dear God, help me through this.

Gee thanks, Doc, for filling me with poison. Someday we'll look back at chemo as we now look back at leeches and bloodletting— it's barbaric. Take a dying person and poison her. Lousy idea, except for the fact that it apparently works. Okay, fine. Thanks for poisoning me so I might live.

"I have an idea," I said. "Let's play a game, and I'll win. Pain, you try to break me, and I won't let you. I'll sit here and not give in to you for thirty seconds. I'll will myself to not feel you, until I can't stand it anymore; then I'll give in and sob. Okay, go!" For thirty seconds I fought it and felt all right, encouraging myself with, "Don't feel it. Don't feel it. Don't give in; you're stronger than this is. Stay angry, stay strong, keep fighting!" It focused my energy to fight something evil off of myself. I kept thinking of battling spirits and principalities.

After about twenty-five seconds, I told myself to try extending it to sixty seconds. Sometimes I could go that long; sometimes I couldn't. Throughout the day I'd repeat my vow to fight. Sometimes I'd go for two minutes, sometimes more, but I'd always have to give myself thirty-second pep talks, thinking of nothing else. Eventually, I could stave off the pain for up to a half hour. It was exhausting. I was worn out, but I couldn't remember being in pain afterward. It got me through the day, and I'd say, "Screw you, pain, screw you, Satan. I've got God on my side."

Thank you, God, for giving me the strength, just enough, to win every day.

THINGS WE NEVER WANTED TO LEARN ABOUT PAIN

A chiropractor once said to me, "David, are you a military veteran? You have such a high pain tolerance!" I actually think I'm a wimp when it comes to physical pain. I've never had a broken bone. I've never had a serious illness. Fortunately, I've never personally experienced childbirth.

But there is no pain like watching your child suffer and not being able to make it stop. In fact, that's how they break the tough guys in the movies. The hero resists all kinds of torture until they bring in someone precious to him and threaten to inflict pain on the one he loves. Then the hero caves in.

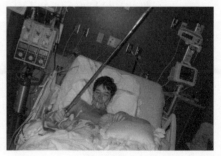

Ian the warrior

I can only imagine the pain my son experienced with that tumor pressing on his organs with unrelenting force. Drugs helped, but one day even heavy narcotics didn't seem to dull the pain of having a tube the size of his little finger inserted between his ribs to drain fluids. By

35

the time that tube was inserted, I'd been at Ian's side 24/7 in the ICU for more than two weeks, taking a graduate course on pain.

As Ian slept, in the darkness I journaled on the meanings of pain:

- **Pain is a gift**. Renee has a book titled *Pain: The Gift Nobody Wants*. It's written by a physician who explains the value of pain and how we'd be in deep trouble without this God-given warning system. What if Ian had felt no searing back pain that took us to the ER? The lethal tumor would have grown unchecked and killed him within weeks.
- **Pain increases our capacity.** When I was searching for God as a teenager, I read a book by a Lebanese mystic named Kahlil Gibran. I remember he said that pain is the tool God uses to carve out the crucible of our hearts so they have a greater capacity for joy. It's clear to me that cancer is developing depth in Ian beyond his years. Before my eyes, he is becoming the young man I long for him to be.
- **Pain brings us together.** Picture every member of your body responding to your fingers caught in a slammed car door: your voice box screaming, your face grimacing, your knees buckling, your mind working out solutions, your other hand trying to help. This is a remarkable picture of how the body of Christ around the world is responding to Ian's pain, to **our** pain.
- **Pain opens our eyes to see God in a new way.** As I watch Ian suffer, I think of our heavenly Father watching the agony of His Son on the cross. Surely His heart writhed in agony. Surely He wanted to stop His Son's pain. When Ian winces and cries out, I leap out of sleep to do everything in my power to help. Often there is little I can do. What courage and love the Father showed in withholding His angels, restraining His power, and allowing His Son to suffer for us. My view of the cross is forever changed. My view of pain is forever changed.

THE REST OF THE STORY

It's so easy to allow pain to lead us into despair. But despair always presumes that we know what God is going to do next. Despair presumes that we know how the story ends.

What if you met Joseph, from the book of Genesis, toward the middle of his life? He's obscenely wealthy; he has a stunning wife and lovely children. His boss does essentially whatever Joseph tells him to do. He seems to have it made. It would appear that his whole life had been handed to him on a silver platter. But we know the rest of the story. Joseph was beaten up, thrown into a pit, sold to slave traders, framed, and locked away in prison. There he was betrayed and forgotten for years. Painful betrayal seemed like the theme of his life. A snapshot of Joseph at the pinnacle of his life would not have shown the preface of pain that prepared him for his destiny. Truly great people often have a preface of pain. God often places His choice ones in the fire and on the anvil, hammering them into what they will need to be in the need of the hour.

Everyone experiences pain. The making of people of destiny is often about how they respond to the anvil of pain. It's not about what happens to you; it's about how you respond.

DREAMS AND NIGHTMARES

In March 2008, after a month in pediatric intensive care, Ian was able to come home. But the nightmare continued with intensive chemotherapy multiple days every week and dozens of blood transfusions. Then one night Ian was seized with pain even more intense than he'd known before. Ironically, the dozens of blood transfusions had grown a gallstone that brought on pain even more intense than childbirth.

And I was in Mexico, unable to do anything to help. A person like me normally wants to figure out what to *do* about a problem. Once again I was facing a problem I could not solve. What could I *do*? What are we called to do in the midst of tribulation?

I am finding answers to these questions in Romans 5, James 1, and 2 Corinthians 4. The answers in these passages can be frustrating, but they're beginning to make more sense to me.

- "We also *exult* in our tribulations, knowing that tribulation brings about perseverance; and perseverance, proven character; and proven character, hope; and hope does not disappoint, because the love of God has been poured out within our hearts through the Holy Spirit who was given to us" (Romans 5:3-5, NASB, emphasis added).
- "*Consider it all joy*, my brethren, when you encounter various trials, knowing that the testing of your faith produces endurance. And let endurance have its perfect result, so that you may be perfect and complete, lacking in nothing" (James 1:2-4, NASB, emphasis added).

"We do not lose heart" (2 Corinthians 4:1, NIV). Rather than losing heart—which has been a constant temptation—these passages call us to cling to what we know. We are called to focus on what is unseen, what is not obvious now but will be prominent in eternity. And we are called to *consider it all joy* when we encounter various trials (James 1) and to *exult* in our tribulations (Romans 5). That is, we are called to take pride in our suffering, to glory in it, to revel in it. We are called to lean into it and embrace it.

Although it was unintentional, I guess that's what I had been trying to do as we walked the cancer road. I turned to the Truth again and again, clinging to it and meditating on it. That is vital, because the truth is not where our feelings or circumstances tend to take us when we're in pain. And I fell into sharing my wrestlings with Truth through e-mail and our website. The words *exult*, *glory*, *revel*, and *joy* seem over the top. They are not the words I would choose to describe what I was doing. But in retrospect, they can describe it. I was putting our suffering out there for the world to see. Rather than hiding it, or suffering secretly and alone, I shared it with anyone who would listen. And in a strange and wonderful way, that brought joy and grace flowing into our lives.

So I was *doing* my part.

But what was God doing? What was His intent in all of this?

- **Perseverance, proven character, and hope.** "We also exult in our tribulations, knowing that *tribulation brings about perseverance*; and perseverance, *proven character*; and proven character, *hope*; and hope does not disappoint, because the love of God has been poured out within our hearts through the Holy Spirit who was given to us" (Romans 5:3-5, NASB, emphasis added). Tribulations are God's standard operating procedure for developing these qualities in our lives. Paul was so convinced of this, and so eager to acquire those qualities, that he actually exulted in tribulations. I remember my son Wesley coming home from crew practice, saying, "That was a great practice! Three guys actually threw up!" I walked away shaking my head. But that's the kind of attitude that eventually led them into the national finals; they wanted it that badly. How badly do I want proven character?

- **Wholeness, completion, and integration.** "Consider it all joy, my brethren, when you encounter various trials, knowing that the testing of your faith produces endurance. And let endurance have its perfect result, *so that you may be perfect and complete*, lacking in nothing" (James 1:2-4, NASB, emphasis added). James had the same idea as Paul. They both had learned from experience that trials and testing are at the heart of how God makes us into what we long to be. Am I so sick of hypocrisy and inconsistencies in my life that joy rises in my heart when I see God doing surgery on me?

- **Manifestation of the life of Jesus.** "But we have this treasure in earthen vessels, so that the surpassing greatness of the power will be of God and not from ourselves; we are afflicted in every way, but not crushed; perplexed, but not despairing; persecuted, but not forsaken; struck down, but not destroyed; always carrying about in the body the dying of Jesus, so that the life of Jesus also may be manifested in our body. For we who live are constantly being delivered over to death for Jesus' sake, *so that the life of Jesus also may be manifested in our mortal flesh*" (2 Corinthians 4:7-11, NASB, emphasis added).

Paul made it clear that it is through affliction, perplexity, mistreatment, and even death that the life of Jesus becomes visible in us. God uses difficulties to lead us out of our petty preoccupation with ourselves and into experiencing His life. I'd had premonitions that big trouble was ahead, but this wasn't merely theory and theology anymore. Now we were taking the test. Now we'd see if all I'd said was really true. And well-designed tests reveal what is really in us. So there we were—living the dream! Ha! I guess that dreams and nightmares sleep together.

God was working out proven character and wholeness, and making the life of Jesus become more and more visible in and through us. That's the dream. That's the deepest longing of my heart.

But that dream has always come with a price tag that frightens most of us away.

DOMESTICATED DISCIPLES

Recently I've been watching the gospel of John dramatized on video. In a fresh way I've been noticing how Jesus called His disciples way, *way* out of their comfort zones. They were not following Him to join the Rotary Club to advance their social standing or career. This was no fraternity rush promising fun parties every weekend. No, this was a war zone. He was leading them into a battle rife with live ammunition.

As He led them further and further from safe harbor, He also called them to trust Him completely with and for everything. He can be trusted, but not to leave you in comfortable self-sufficiency.

One way I express this as I follow Him today is through this prayer that I return to several times a week:

> Lord, You are always completely holy, powerful, and loving, and together those qualities make You worthy of my absolute trust. I do trust You, and once again I turn to You with the longings and anxieties of my heart because Your motives are always pure, You never fail to do what You promise, and You always have my best interests in mind. So I let go of all other gods and idols to which I have looked for life: ideas, appetites, desires, dreams, positions, reputations, methods, people, and things. I confess here and now that it is all about You, God, and not about me, my ideas of what should be, my fulfillment, or my comfort, convenience, or control. For You are the Hero of this story.

Pain is a threat to personal safety, and we are a culture obsessed with personal safety. I gag at the motto of one of our local Christian radio stations: "Safe for the whole family!" I know what they're getting at, and I also work hard at providing a morally protected environment for my kids. But in the larger sense, is following Jesus safe? Most of Jesus' original followers were violently executed much like their Leader. The cloud of witnesses (literally, martyrs) mentioned in Hebrews 12:1 must see us as so domesticated.

In C. S. Lewis's famed CHRONICLES OF NARNIA series, when the children hear about Aslan, the great lion, they ask, "Is he safe?" "No," they're told, "but he is good." Similarly, Renee and I had to move beyond looking for God to keep our son safe and trust that He was working for Ian's good. That meant we had to let him live his life.

Even though Ian's immune system was at a low point, one Saturday morning we hiked up a canyon to one of our favorite family destinations, the Punch Bowls. As Ian was scampering over the rocks, he slipped and fell into the microbe-filled water below and began bleeding. With such low blood counts, would the bleeding stop? (Yes.) Would he get an infection? (He developed a low-grade fever with few white blood cells to fight it, but it turned out okay.) Did we make a mistake as parents? I don't think so. Our son needed to live life.

We don't let three-year-olds handle sharp knives. We don't let our kids ride with teenage drivers. And we wouldn't leave a thirteen-year-old with cancer to do whatever he likes, because the consequences could be too severe. But we didn't want to strangle him with overprotection either. We wanted him to be free to live life all out. Isn't that where Jesus led His disciples?

LIFE IN ANOTHER WORLD

Nine months after Ian's initial diagnosis, the Make-A-Wish Foundation sent our family to Hawaii to fulfill Ian's wish to scuba dive around a coral reef. It was a spectacular vacation for all of us. We especially enjoyed snorkeling. That was a feat for me because I'm generally very uncomfortable swimming in deep water, having nearly drowned as a boy. But I really wanted to experience the clear blue waters and brilliantly colored coral and fish. So with God's help, I kept overcoming my fears. As I swam, I was constantly pushing down my anxiety and actually having the time of my life.

At the end of our first day in the water, my fears were pushed to the limit. We were given the opportunity to snorkel at night with huge manta rays, seven to ten feet across. All my natural instincts held me back from jumping into that black water. But the thrill and anticipation spurred me on. Then I came face-to-face with my first manta ray, swooping up from the depths to the powerful light held by our guide to attract plankton that the rays eat. I shoved down my fear as he opened his mouth wide, coming toward me out of the dark and sweeping within inches of my face again and again in a magnificent underwater ballet.

That was not "fun." But I would not have missed it for anything. It was a thrill. It was an encounter with everyday life in another world.

God's way is to lead us out into deeper water. It is there that we experience the thrill of what only He can do, where we'll drown unless He comes through for us.

Pain is the gift that God gives to usher us into the life and joy and freedom and peace and "everyday life in another world" that He intends for us.

LIVING IN SPITE OF THE PAIN

From Linda's Journal
April 2009

Last month I began my fourth round of chemo in nine years, so it should be no big deal by now. Ha! Everything aches, even my teeth and eyelashes. My brain isn't tired, but my body can barely move. If this was pre-2000, I'd stay in bed, drink hot soup, and expect to be babied. But it's not. It's 2009, and I'm not sick. I just have cancer. Compared to the uninitiated person I was nine years ago, who could barely function through the pain, I don't really consider it that bad anymore. It's all a matter of perspective. The drugs are much better now, less debilitating, but I'm also a veteran of living with pain. It no longer controls me. My response is no longer a desperate, "God, please make it stop." Now I say, "Oh, that again. I don't like it but I'll get through it, and in the meantime, I have other things to do."

I hate to complain about my pain when Ian has to endure so much more. The thing is, I feel blessed to suffer so little in comparison at this point. It didn't used to feel like a blessing. It used to feel like crap. Now I just walk through it and don't want any sympathy. In a strange way, the pain has made me stronger than I was. Last week, I had chemo on Wednesday, then woke up early Thursday to drive nine hours to Kentucky to help our daughter move from a third-floor apartment. Up and down, moving and cleaning. All of a sudden, I thought I was going to die right then and there. "Morgan," I said, "this is not a complaint. In fact, I think I might be bragging, but how many fifty-eight-year-old women do you know who would have chemo one day, drive nine hours the next, and immediately help their daughter move out of a third-story apartment? What is wrong with me?"

What's "wrong" is that I no longer let the pain stop me. It spurs me on to do better things because God has strengthened me, even though I don't always know it at the time. "But the Lord stood at my side and gave me strength, so that through me the message might be fully proclaimed and all the Gentiles might hear it. And I was delivered from the lion's mouth" (2 Timothy 4:17, NIV).

I just keep getting back into the ring. I'll keep swinging until my arms give out. And that will take awhile.

EMBRACING THE GIFT

From Linda's Journal
July 7, 2009

Today I went to my summer prayer group. It's a casual and fun time, giving us a chance to share our burdens and joys with others and to intercede for our friends. It's one of the rare times in my life when I don't feel like an alien; here, I belong.

After our meetings, one woman types up the requests. Each person usually has one or two lines of summary. Today mine was sixteen lines long. Geez. I must be a mess.

More than one person thanked God today for "Linda's great and positive attitude about her life." Ha! I would have felt admired except that I felt like a fraud. They should live in this house and have to put up with me for a day! During my morning walk down by the river, before I even went to the

Linda with her children during chemo

prayer group, I found myself having to apologize to God for being such a lousy person. I complain. I whine. I'm not nice. I'm judgmental. I can be a real pain. But fortunately, only my husband hears my woes. He suffers while I get it off my chest; then I'm fine again.

Tonight I realize that I've been given a gift. If I had never known how bad life can be, I'd never have found out how wonderful life really is. Life was fine before but was somewhat mundane and meaningless for years. I had happy times but nothing that compared with knowing God personally as I do now. The contrast is infinite. The bad seems so meaningless now compared to the good. Or as Paul said, "What is more, I consider everything a loss compared to the surpassing greatness of knowing Christ Jesus my Lord, for whose sake I have lost all things" (Philippians 3:8, NIV).

A customer once gave me a copy of the old children's book, *Pollyanna*, saying it reminded her of me. I was momentarily appalled and tried not to gag. I hate sappy. She begged me not to be insulted, saying it was meant

If you are beginning to see how God wants to use the gift of pain to help us grow, then consider visiting *dontwastethepain.com* to build on what you are learning in this book.

There you can share your story or listen in on how others are growing through their pain. There you can move beyond reading Truths to making them your own. And you or your small group can join a virtual small group led by a mentor. Don't just read. Take the next step!

as a compliment. She loved that I was always making jokes, looking up rather than down, and never letting the cancer depress me. She said it inspired her to be the same way about her own trials. Well, that "looking up" thing is straight from God; it doesn't come naturally. And that's the gift.

I'm no Pollyanna and I'm no hero, but I'm thankful that God lets me see reality. I don't do that on my own. God does it in me. Cancer is not what Satan hoped it would be. Rather than a curse, for me it's truly a gift, and God reminds me of that over and over again.

QUESTIONS FOR REFLECTION

▶ How do you really feel about your pain at this point? (Be completely honest with yourself.)

▶ How do you feel about this statement: "It's not about what happens to you; it's about how you respond"?

▶ What gifts do you think God may be trying to give you through pain?

CHAPTER 3

OXYGEN

Sometimes God uses pain to press the eject button on our comfortable lives, suddenly launching our sense of control into thin air. We may aspire to live surrendered lives, but it is so unfamiliar, so unnatural, so fearful that under normal circumstances, we end up shrinking back from it. I would have said I was living a surrendered life prior to Ian's diagnosis, but it took an extended stay in the pediatric ICU to push me into the type of moment-by-moment dependence that God expects us to live.

Late one night after two days of nonstop, life-threatening crisis, I sat down beside Ian's bed to write in my journal:

> If there was any sense of putting our confidence in anything but God here, that confidence has been pushed aside by harsh realities. Thankfully, God does not deal in probabilities. He does not read survival rates from medical journals to calculate what is likely to happen with Ian. God does not *probably* work for our good. God is not *probably* going to succeed in doing whatever He chooses. God *always* works for our good, and He *never* fails. Yet our emotions are caught in the sometimes frightening intersection of faith and living in a broken world. So we pray and cling to the One who transcends all of this.

I was putting on my oxygen mask. You know the routine. Every time we step onto a plane, the flight attendant briefs us, just in case. How often have I dozed through those safety briefings? But this was no drill. My son could really die. And I desperately needed to access the "oxygen," the peace and grace and wisdom found only in Jesus.

A NEW WAY OF BREATHING

There is something deep within us that resists living in moment-by-moment dependence on God. We fight it—hard.

A compelling scene in the movie *The Abyss* has stuck with me over the years. The entire film takes place deep under water. The survival of the underwater crew depends on the captain diving deeper than conventional equipment will allow. He has to use experimental equipment that enables him to "breathe" liquid oxygen. Everything in him fights against what seems so abnormal. The camera zooms in on his face as his helmet fills with liquid. His comrade assures him it will be okay: "Remember, you breathed liquid for nine months in your mother's womb!"[1] Still, you see the terror on his face as he "inhales" the liquid, literally drowning himself to survive. For a moment he convulses violently because it's so unnatural. Then he recovers and begins breathing the liquid, typing on a computer, "This is weird. You should try it!"

That can be what it feels like to relinquish control and enter into moment-by-moment surrender to God. It can feel like dying. No wonder God often has to force our hand through our circumstances. I remember Jesus saying something about dying so that we can live: "I tell you the truth, unless a kernel of wheat falls to the ground and dies, it remains only a single seed. But if it dies, it produces many seeds" (John 12:24, NIV).

I was learning to breathe deeply. I was learning to breathe the supernatural air that I was designed to breathe. I was learning to be carried along by grace in new ways I had not known. We can live for weeks without food and for days without water. We can only live for minutes without oxygen. We are designed to take in fresh oxygen all the time. Without it we die. We were also designed to abide in Christ so completely that apart from Him we can do nothing, not even for a few minutes. "I am the vine; you are the branches. If a man remains in me and I in him, he will bear much fruit; apart from me you can do nothing" (John 15:5, NIV). Although it sounds weird, we should all try it.

COCKY DISCIPLES

One of the greatest obstacles to a surrendered life is our own self-sufficiency. As I experience God's faithfulness, I tend to misconstrue it as my own faithfulness and strength and ability. I become like Hezekiah, who was "marvelously helped until he was strong" (2 Chronicles 26:15, NASB). I become like the disciples, who got used to God doing miracles through them and became cocky.

I can identify with the desperate father in Mark 9. Because his son had suffered so much, he tried to bring him to Jesus. But Jesus was away, so he approached Jesus' disciples. They attempted to do what they had done with such spectacular success before. But this time miracles eluded them.

The father's desperation roared. Then, finally, Jesus Himself appeared. The father's fears tumbled out through his words: "If You can do anything, take pity on us and help us!" (verse 22, NASB).

Jesus' indignation roared. "O unbelieving generation, how long shall I be with you? How long shall I put up with you? . . . 'If You can?' All things are possible to him who believes" (verses 19,23, NASB).

The father whimpered, "I do believe; help my unbelief" (verse 24, NASB).

Then Jesus healed the boy. And a few minutes later, in private, He taught His humiliated disciples a life lesson: "This kind cannot come out by anything but prayer" (verse 29, NASB). In other words, it requires complete dependence on God's abilities, not our own.

The disciples had healed many people before, and they assumed they could do it again. They had gotten cocky. This self-confidence apparently came on them easily because they had not maintained a posture of humble reliance on the Father, demonstrated through the regular discipline of prayer. But Jesus, always dependent on the Father, was ready for the challenge.

That's where we want to live—in complete dependence on and surrender to the Spirit of God so Jesus can freely live through us. Something in us wants to live in the supernatural zone, where only God in us can live. Something in us needs to depend on God like we depend on oxygen. It's so contrary to the world's message, which says pull yourself together and gut out the pain through your own strength. Linda was learning to breathe, and she was teaching me.

DON'T FORGET TO BE WEAK

Letter from Linda
March 2008

David and Linda

David, don't forget to be weak. When Mom and Dad died, you became the "strong male figure" in the Lyons family. You are a dad to seven, a leader in your field, someone whom many count on for strength. Don't forget to be weak. Don't refuse to just give up on being able to help Ian. Don't forget to get out of the way and lie down and be a little child. You know all this, but perhaps you need to hear it from someone you love and trust—and someone you know has been there.

"For when I am weak, then I am strong" (2 Corinthians 12:10, NIV).

Giving up and having no hope is not what I'm saying. But do give up having any influence, any control, any say in the outcome, any power at all. It's God who decides whether we can do any of those things. Don't just say it, wish it, or assume God will intervene because it's what you believe; it has to be total emptiness and submission in you. You have to "die" in it. I promise you, Dave, that it will be the most peaceful place you can be.

These are not "religious" words. This is a miracle that your big sister learned the hard way. I finally said, "Fine. I hate this, and I think I hate You right now, and I bleepin' give up. Do whatever You want. Nothing could be worse than fighting this fight, so You have to take over." Or something like that. I just gave up and told Him to do whatever He wanted with me. I was empty. And then the peace that has ruled my life came into me, and I survived. Nothing can hurt me now.

I have a lot to learn from my big sister. Her radical love and surrender inspire me. A year before our cancer journey began, Linda had already figured out a lot about living a surrendered life.

From Linda's Journal
March 2007

I'm not comfortable with people who tell me how "brave" I am or how they can't believe how well I'm handling all this. If they only knew that it's not me who is brave. Friends, you know it's not me; it's the Holy Spirit, who's acting in me. There are moments (only moments?) I just hate all this. I'm so tired of dealing with it, but somehow that almost never comes out. It just passes away as if it never haunted me, because it never seems worth it to complain. Therefore, it makes me squirm when people think more of me than I deserve.

I nearly passed out from weakness when I arrived for chemo this morning and scared my nurse by collapsing into my chair. Elaine turned me around toward the exit door and said, "Get out!" Okay, maybe she said, "Oh dear, Linda, your body is not strong enough to go through this today, so go home and rest." So I did, right after I went to Jo-Ann Fabric, Trader Joe's, and Giant Food. Some things just have to get done.

Am I really the only one who wakes up every morning flat on the floor, grabbing onto Christ's ankle to pull me up? Is everyone else supernatural or something? Actually, it's not me who grabs His ankle. It's not me who grabs onto Him for strength. It's Him who constantly holds onto me, no matter what I do. I'm always "in His grip" as my dear friend Nan says. Even when I let go due to frustration, lack of faith, or weariness, He never lets go of me. I could be unconscious, and He'd still have me.

WOBBLY

God doesn't want us to merely take a few breaths of complete dependence, then return to the surface. He wants us to learn to live there, depending on Him for everything. It's relatively easy to "gear up" for a crisis and to depend on God when we really have no other options. So sometimes our suffering is sustained, because God intends for us to come out of these crises into a new way of living, a lifestyle of dependence.

I wrote this the day we brought Ian home from the hospital:

> Strangely, with Ian home and feeling better today, I'm feeling kind of down. Why is that? Maybe I'm just suffering withdrawal of the adrenaline rush from these weeks of constant crises. Maybe I miss feeling so desperately needed. Maybe now that the urgency of this crisis is receding a bit, I'm facing other life realities again. Maybe everyday responsibilities seem mundane after living in 24/7 "life-saving" mode for so long. Maybe I'm just tired. Maybe the Enemy is trying to attack me while I'm weak

and vulnerable. Maybe it's all of that.

Lord, it's as if You are gently lowering my feet to the ground again after carrying me in Your arms for so long. Just like Ian's legs were wobbly after being in bed for so long, I guess my everyday faith legs may be a bit wobbly. You may soon have to pick me up again, Lord. I don't know what this next round of chemotherapy will bring.

Father, all of this reminds me how I need to depend on You for everything all the time. Times like this help us to see things as they really are, stripping away our illusions of self-sufficiency and self-determination, melting away superficial values, clearing our minds, and invigorating our spirits.

Trials are intended to develop perseverance, endurance, staying power, the ability to continue living in complete dependence. I want to go to that place even when the trial has passed. I want a new normal.

YBNRML

A friend of mine used to have a license plate that read "YBNRML." (Translation: Why be normal?) Good question! Normal can be sick. Normal can be toxic. Normal can miss real Life.

In some ways I fear normal. During the first two months of Ian's cancer walk, we experienced extraordinary love and support. We were carried along on the prayer arms of our friends and family. But then the big splash of attention receded, as it should. We wondered if an ebbing tide of corporate faith would leave us stranded on the beach.

Here's what Linda had to say about that:

> Yes, the new normal is tiresome, and we feel weary from it along with you. On the other hand, the new you and the new Ian and the new everyone else in your family can handle

more now than any of you could two months ago. That's something. It makes any future "new normals" less scary. You know now what you are capable of handling, or, more realistically, what you can endure with God's grace.

You asked, "Will an ebbing tide of corporate faith leave us stranded on the beach?" No more than the natural ocean's waves "strand" a beautiful stone on the beach after it's been beaten, then smoothed by the sea to its new place of perfection and beauty on some distant shore. You are different, worn, changed, even strengthened, with amazing opportunities on that new shore. But you are not stranded. Still, it's going to feel like that at times. It can be very easy to come to rely on the notes and calls of others to build us up and remind us of what God is doing. But it's not the affirmation of friends that gives us the newfound strength—I don't even need to finish this sentence. You know the Source of your strength.

Normal seems like an old friend, until God interrupts. I used to always print this on the cover of our annual ministry plan: "Plan your work, and work your plan. But God may do the best things as interruptions to your plans." Cancer certainly interrupted our plans.

One morning in the midst of our ordeal, I read in Mark 5 about a leader whose life was interrupted by his child's life-threatening illness. Jairus was a leader in his faith community (the local synagogue). He would never have chosen such an interruption from leading his people. Yet without it, he may never have experienced God's presence in such a powerful way. He had to become desperate before he could really experience God.

There is desperation throughout Mark 5. Legion, Jairus, and the woman who had hemorrhaged for twelve years were all desperate. They were living far from the normalcy most of us crave and defend. Yet their desperation is what caused them to encounter God in an extraordinary way.

So should we seek crises? It seems like some people do. But the lesson for me is to see my desperate need in everyday life. I easily become content with living a merely human life. In 1 Corinthians 3 Paul chided the Corinthians for living like "mere men" because they had become accustomed to living in unloving ways, careless about holiness, unaware of others' needs. They were living out of their flesh rather than out of the Spirit of God inside them.

I can fall into the trap of living that way, too. I can merely enjoy the anemic American dream, living without the Life of God flowing through me. But God cares too much for me to let me stay there, and that's usually when pain steps in to do its work. In his second letter to the Corinthians, Paul wrote how affliction in its many forms has a purpose: "So that the life of Jesus also may be manifested in our mortal flesh" (verse 11, NASB). (Read 2 Corinthians 4:7-11 again.)

Frankly, I don't even like myself when I'm not living in the Spirit. On my own I'm cranky, impatient, and harsh. I've often said that if you experience gentleness from me, you know there must be a God. It just doesn't come naturally to me. But it does come *supernaturally*. So I am desperate every day—I have this desperate need to be filled with the holy and living Spirit of Jesus. Pain opens my eyes to that desperation. Sometimes it's the pain of unpleasant consequences from my selfish behavior. Sometimes it's the pain of tragedy that has invaded my space. Either way, whether I'm aware of it or not, I am in desperate need.

Are we desperate enough to "Live Jesus"?[2] Or will we be rocked to sleep by normalcy?

LIVE IN TODAY

Six weeks after Ian was diagnosed, Linda wrote this to him:

> It's a bit late to advise this now, but being anxious is not worth it. When I flew out to see you last month, I had three things to consider:

1. My CA-125 was too high, and I was supposedly coming home from seeing you to begin another round of chemo.
2. I was scheduled to have a suspicious mole evaluated for cancer by a dermatologist.
3. My recent mammogram showed a new dark spot on my breast, and I had to have a second mammogram with a sonogram.

As I was getting ready to leave, I told Steve that I probably had ovarian cancer, skin cancer, and breast cancer. Then we laughed and decided that either life sucks or I'd be fine.

I like to think I made a conscious decision to be at peace, but really, God did it for me by not allowing me to worry. I spent approximately, let's see, NO time worrying about any of it while with you. And look what happened. No chemo for now. The mole was fine. The spot on my breast disappeared by the second mammogram. So . . . nothing. What a waste of energy if I'd worried. How miserable I'd have been if, like most people, I was consumed with the "what ifs." After all this time, it's easier than it once was to have that attitude. It's not something that comes naturally.

The way to get there is to live in today. Don't worry about tomorrow for tomorrow has enough trouble of its own. I read that somewhere—and you know where! Just live in today, and don't waste time thinking of the "what ifs" of the future. Pretend you're in heaven when it will always be today.

"Come on in," Linda was saying to my son. "The oxygen is fine!"

Looking back on it now, apparently Ian took Linda's advice to heart. As I reread her letter, I realize how deeply Linda's encouragement and example shaped Ian's responses. At Ian's funeral, his older brother Wesley said this:

Ian had a very serious "Don't sweat the small stuff" policy—and the extraordinary thing about that was that he decided cancer fell in the "small stuff" category. He was so convinced that cancer wasn't worth stressing about that he would tell other kids at the oncology unit that they should "get over it" and that cancer just "wasn't that big of a deal." To an extent that was troublesome to his caretakers; he just would not complain. I never heard him complain; those who were with him all the time say that it was an extreme rarity—and I don't think I need to go through a list of the painful, uncomfortable, annoying, disheartening things he endured. He did not sit around and let things come at him or pine away about what was happening to him. He went after life. He lived "a bloc" (French for "all out").

JUST BREATHE

Ian now breathes the heavenly oxygen we are all designed to breathe. And us?

As I write it's been three months since Ian died, so I'm very much in the midst of grief. When people ask how I am doing—and actually want an answer—I say, "I'm being carried along." Many days I really feel like there is just one set of footprints in the sand, and they are not mine. I often awake and sigh, *Lord, You are going to have to carry me again today.* Through the day my emotional margins are thinner than before, keeping me from wandering off into self-sufficiency. Earlier this week I received hard news, and it threw me. But I think that falling into His arms and letting Him carry me came more easily than it has in the past. And being carried is not a bad place to be.

Will I continue to embrace this way of living? When grief recedes, will I return to my default settings of self-sufficiency? I hope not. I don't want all this pain to be wasted.

As I look at Linda now—in contrast to the Linda I knew before she got cancer—I believe it is possible to keep breathing heavenly oxygen even after the intensity of the crisis has subsided. It reminds me of Jesus telling us to *remain* in the Vine, so that the Life of God keeps flowing into and through us every day.

Letter from Linda to David
July 2009

Steve and I are going on nine years of living with cancer, an impressive amount of time considering my original diagnosis. As we walked along the river recently, he said, "It's no longer you and me, it's us. We're one; we're in this together." He was referring to an appointment next week for me to see a specialist in Baltimore.

I had planned to go alone and was puzzled when Steve seemed offended that I hadn't assumed he'd go with me. When he reminded

Steve and Linda

me of our journey together, I realized how wrong it was to even think of not including him in this. The thing is, I have so completely let go of worrying about any of this that I'm almost too casual about it. I don't dwell on it. I find myself resting in God's care, and I don't think much about the details of my health care or my future. Better to look outward than dwell on me. God is in control.

Two women in my Bible study have struggled with anxiety recently over husbands who were diagnosed with prostate cancer. They have been emotionally spent, and we have lifted them up in prayer—not only for the healing of the men they love, but especially for the women to be at peace. So I wondered what was "wrong" with me when I had no fears or worry when Steve also had to be tested for the same disease. I never even thought to mention it to them.

Didn't I care? Of course I do, but why start to worry at this stage of my life? And after several weeks, we learned he's fine anyway.

What would have been the point of frantic worrying, other than to prove I don't quite trust God? Why worry today when "tomorrow will worry about itself. Each day has enough trouble of its own" (Matthew 6:34, NIV)? God gives me my very breath "because he himself gives all men life and breath and everything else" (Acts 17:25, NIV). It is by His oxygen that I breathe and live in peace.

QUESTIONS FOR REFLECTION

- ▶ At what points in your life have you found yourself most desperately clinging to God?
- ▶ How are you feeling about accepting whatever God might have in mind for you?
- ▶ What things keep you from breathing God's oxygen all the time—even when you're not in pain?

CHAPTER 4

THE RAGGED
EDGE OF FAITH

Faith matters. It matters a lot.

I think the cloud of witnesses described in Hebrews is watching when we are being tested, to see if we will respond with the same faith that carried them.

> Therefore, since we have so great a cloud of witnesses surrounding us, let us also lay aside every encumbrance and the sin which so easily entangles us, and let us run with endurance the race that is set before us. (12:1, NASB)

Hebrews 11, in which we are introduced to some of those witnesses, is known as "The Faith Hall of Fame." There we find names such as Abel, Noah, Moses, Rahab, and, of course, Abraham, the granddaddy of them all. The apostle Paul is surely among those witnesses now. I bet he just can't wait to see how our faith is doing. Even here on earth he was so obsessed with the faith of the Thessalonians that he sent his protégé, Timothy, on an expensive and hazardous journey to have a look.

> For this reason, *when I could stand it no longer,* I sent [Timothy] to find out about your faith. I was afraid that in some way the

tempter might have tempted you and our efforts might have been useless. (1 Thessalonians 3:5, NIV, emphasis added)

Our faith really matters to God. God cares deeply whether we're trusting in Him or in ourselves. He cares so much that He goes to great lengths to arrange faith-stretching opportunities for us. Jesus often provided such opportunities for the disciples—and He wasn't always nice about it. He purposely thrust them into some faith wringers.

As a boy I learned to keep my distance from clothes wringers. Our mother had a 1950s-style washing machine with powerful rollers for wringing water out of the clothes. (I guess it was 1950s style because it *was* the 1950s!) One day I had the job of running the clothes through the wringer and was helping a reluctant shirt on its way when my fingers got caught in the rollers. I learned suddenly that the machine meant business and wondered if Mom would end up hanging me out with the laundry. You can be sure from that day I kept my distance from those rollers.

It's tempting to keep our distance from God, too.

In Matthew 14 we read about Jesus forcing the disciples into the boat. As seasoned fishermen, they knew a storm was coming. But Jesus insisted, "Get into the boat!" So they did. And, sure enough, the storm came. They thought they were going to die. I wonder what they were thinking about their "buddy" Jesus as He let them struggle for hours before casually strolling out on the water to meet them. The disciples were terrified, facing death, and Jesus did what He always does: He showed up and met their real need. Then came the painful debriefing: "You of little faith," said Jesus, "why did you doubt?" (verse 31, NIV).

So why does it surprise us today when God goes to such great lengths in pushing us to the ragged edge of our faith?

During a training program, I was walking with a coleader, and we were musing about how God trains His servants. One of us quipped, "If we designed training programs the way God designs them, they'd throw us in jail!" We were still laughing about that when someone burst in to tell my friend that his son had just been bitten by a rattlesnake. Had there been a tender smile on the Master's face as He listened to us laughing? I don't know. But I do know that God used that "wringer" to build our faith in Him.

EDGE-OF-FAITH MOMENTS

Many of us have said, or at least thought, "It could be worse. At least I don't have cancer." Cancer seems to be what everyone dreads most and works the hardest to avoid. We look with disdain on friends who eat Big Macs and drink diet soda like water. Not us! We're grinding our own wheat and baking our own bread and eating salads—and getting cancer. So what's it like in that place most of us dread? What's it like in the laboratory where faith is so greatly tested? This journal entry, written late at night in a darkened intensive care unit, captures a little of what it feels like on the bleeding edge between self-sufficiency and simple faith.

From David's Journal
February 11, 2008

Being in the hospital with Ian all day and all night for a week now, I've been immersed in the medical world with doctors and nurses and testing and a blizzard of scientific details. From a distance, medical professionals can look so confident, like technicians running a finely tuned and reliable machine. But up close, it's often a messy and confusing business that involves guessing and improvising.

This is no criticism. God has blessed us with a pediatric oncologist with extensive experience. He's a strong believer who is highly regarded by everyone. Besides that, I like and trust him. The night nurse on duty as I write is a winsome believer with extraordinary skills. I deeply appreciate these loving professionals. Yet despite their knowledge and experience, they don't know exactly what's causing the swelling in Ian's arm and haven't been able to stop it. A full week after surgery to implant his portable catheter (port) for chemotherapy, they still don't have the bleeding under control. And none of them can assure us they'll be able to save Ian from this cancer.

This is no academic problem. My son's health and life are on the line. We've been drafted into a game of hardball, and the pitches are coming so fast. It's frightening and upsetting, and we can't just take our ball and go home. We're on the ragged edge of faith here.

Yet it's so simple. Three neighborhood friends came to the hospital to pray for Ian. They are about four and seven and nine. They looked at Ian with wide eyes and simply prayed, "Jesus, please make Ian feel better. Please heal him so that he can play with us again." That's not so complicated.

Medical professionals, a mom, a dad, and children who love Ian—all on the ragged edge of faith looking to the One who knows, who cares, who completely understands, who can heal with a mere word or touch, who loves Ian more than any of us. Our trust is in Him alone.

Edge-of-faith moments may seem spectacular or even glamorous in theory, but in practice, they're just hard and ugly. Refining faith can be messy, dangerous work. But God doesn't take us into these faith-building opportunities lightly or capriciously. They are a key part of His beautiful work in us. Look for that beauty in these glimpses of Linda's faith, being refined and revealed in the midst of her third round of chemotherapy in six years:

From Linda's Journal
January 25, 2007

This week I began a new chemo regimen. The previous one failed to stop the cancer, which was strange because it "should" have been the most effective. Thankfully, Dr. Boice isn't bound by lab results; he watches my body to see how it responds and goes from there. Sometimes I think he knows how I'm doing within moments of seeing me. Perhaps he senses something in my eyes, the tone of my skin, or maybe my voice, that gives him a clue.

If we only looked at the latest blood tests, I'd be a wreck. They're the worst in six years, so thank God I'm not counting on mere numbers to make me better. By now, I know better than to freak out over bad blood counts. I feel fine for the most part, and no tumor has yet been located. It's a mystery! I don't know where God is taking this, but He's the guide, so I'm along for the ride.

Can I whine just a little? More than half of my hair is gone again, and I feel naked without my mane. A little vanity does wonders to keep one's mind off worse things, so be glad I can focus my concerns on that.

Weekly doctor visits and testing are taking a physical and emotional toll, but I'm truly thankful I still feel well—no bone pain, nausea, or other side effects so far. I'm still at my shop full time. I'll work as long as I can but will consider selling if it comes to that. However, I just returned from a road trip to Atlanta where I placed large orders for spring and summer, so I'm planning to be around for a while. If that's not trust in my eventual healing, I don't know what is.

Three months after starting the new chemo, the side effects were taking their toll.

I'm so weary today; I can hardly move. Each time I get chemo, it wears me out a bit more, and this time is no different. The Neulasta keeps my white cell count up, but it causes deep, throbbing bone pain and weariness. The effects are cumulative, so I keep getting wearier. I know that each day of strength comes from our Father, and I know that He answers our prayers. I'm asking you to go to

Him on my behalf right now and ask Him to give me strength today. I'm so tired, but I absolutely know I'll feel better soon.

Cancer arrives like the proverbial mother-in-law who stays too long and asks too many questions.

THE BIG QUESTION

At times, God has seemed to let loose on our family. I've given you a glimpse of the trauma our family experienced before Ian's cancer. Actually, I would say that Ian's cancer has not been the most severe test of my faith. Rather, the trials of the previous four years served to prepare me for the cancer.

Ian's was not your everyday garden-variety cancer. Only fifty people a year get this kind of cancer, and most don't live to tell about it. Remember that by the time it was diagnosed, it had destroyed 95 percent of his bone marrow, and the tumor filling his abdomen was doubling in size every forty-eight hours. Then, just to make things interesting, the week Ian was admitted to the hospital, everyone in my family except me came down with either a severe cold or the flu. They could not come to see us since Ian's immune system was zeroed out. Then the same day Ian was diagnosed, Linda learned that her cancer had returned.

In the midst of all this, I could relate a little better to Job — receiving bad news followed by heartbreaking news with catastrophic news close behind. At least my wife, unlike Job's, was not urging me to curse God and die. But I doubt that God could brag on me like He bragged on Job, saying, "Through all this Job did not sin" (Job 1:22, NASB). No. But Job did become my companion.

The book of Job is all about the Big Question. In the early days of Ian's cancer many suggested that I must be struggling with that question: *Why?* Why would God allow such a tragedy to hit such a child in such a family? The unspoken assertion was, "It's not fair!" And that's exactly where Job and his friends fell off the wagon.

Okay, I'll tip my hand here. Some will object vigorously, but here it is. We all deserve an extremely painful life and death. That's what would be fair. Every breath I breathe, every day I live in health is a gift of mercy and grace. It is not what I deserve. One lie, one act of lust, one sin is all it takes for me to qualify for pain. Unfortunately, our spiritual ancestors led us down this path. But even if they had not, each of us makes our own choices that lead us to the same place.

God is not our debtor. He does not owe us *anything* good. What He owes us is the consequences He promised at the very beginning. Adam and Eve had their chance to choose. God said, "From the tree of the knowledge of good and evil you shall not eat, for in the day that you eat from it you will surely die" (Genesis 2:17, NASB). They ate. And from that day forward "It's not fair" became a very dangerous accusation against God. But let's not blame Adam and Eve. God kept repeating this lesson over and over, illustrating it with bloody sacrifices to show what we deserve and how He wants to rescue us. We're all in this mess together.

We tend to identify more with Job and his friends rather than seeing things from God's perspective. Job just asked honest questions. His friends just said what everyone else was thinking. Then God spoke, and all were stunned into silence.

The LORD said to Job:
"Will the one who contends with the Almighty correct him?
    Let him who accuses God answer him!"
Then Job answered the LORD:
"I am unworthy—how can I reply to you?
    I put my hand over my mouth.
I spoke once, but I have no answer—
    twice, but I will say no more." (Job 40:1-5, NIV)

So forget the big "Why?" question. God is God and I am not. He does not owe me an answer to that question. I love Him anyway. In fact, that shocking reality is what pumps my love for Him. He owes me nothing but loves me so very, very much. I can't take it in. But I know it deeply . . . now. Pain can help us see this more clearly. It seems like God is often gentler with those whose knowledge of His love and goodness has not yet grown strong. But when He sees that His saplings are strong enough to endure the wind, He plants them out where they can become oaks of righteousness that withstand the storms of life.

But we're left with something else, the Scary Question that we'd rather leave unspoken.

THE SCARY QUESTION

It seems important to people to say that God would never hurt us. That line of thinking concerns me deeply, because it sets up people to become disillusioned with God — or with those who teach such things. It also concerns me because it requires disregarding so much of how God reveals Himself in the Scriptures. And it touched an open nerve for me as we walked through so much pain with our son. Had God forgotten us? No! Was God mad at us? I don't think so.

The answer is found in something that has become more and more precious to me: seasoned trust. Naive trust says, "God will always work out things the way I want them to be." Notice the big "I" in that sentence. But seasoned trust says, "God might hurt me, but I trust Him anyway." Why would I trust Him anyway? Because I've seen so much of His love and goodness in the Scriptures and in my own life. The torrents of pain have to flow around those immovable rocks.

In the midst of these questions, I landed in Isaiah 26: "The steadfast of mind You will keep in perfect peace, because he trusts in You" (verse 3, NASB).

These familiar words come in a context I had not noticed before — a whirlwind of God's judgments falling on the nations that have turned their backs on their Creator. So this steadfastness and perfect peace come in the midst of great turmoil and distress. As the world seems to be coming apart at the seams, the steadfast one is waiting for God Himself—at night when things can seem so dark and hopeless, and the truth can seem like a distant memory.

> Indeed, while following the way of Your judgments, O LORD,
> We have waited for You eagerly;
> Your name, even Your memory, is the desire of our souls.
> At night my soul longs for You,
> Indeed, my spirit within me seeks You diligently;
> For when the earth experiences Your judgments
> The inhabitants of the world learn righteousness. (verses 8-9, NASB)

What the steadfast one remembers of God—that is the desire of his soul. The world around him is groaning and shrieking with agony, but he is learning. He's learning righteousness. To others, the world may seem like a chaotic mess. But to the steadfast one, it is a context for learning what is most important. Why? Because he trusts in God.

Trust is the cord that keeps him leashed to the mast as the hurricane tears everything else from its moorings. Trust quiets the voices of anger and fear, and allows him to consider that God is working for his good. Trust keeps hope alive, and even eager, as it waits. Trust nurtures and protects one's memory of what is true and right. Trust protects one's longing for God when it might have been extinguished. Trust strengthens one's spirit to keep looking for God when He seems so far away.

Will God hurt me? Sometimes. But only out of love and wisdom. A dear friend calls Him the "Blessed Controller of All Things." She has often said, "God is too loving to be unkind and too wise to make any mistakes." Right now that friend is suffering in a nursing home with dementia. I hope she can remember this truth until the end. She is living on the ragged edge of faith.

DOUBTS

Ian's big brother Wes

Every one of us has to deal with our doubts. One of our big roles as parents is to help our children walk through theirs—and when we do, sometimes we end up confronting our own.

Ian's big brother Wes is a larger-than-life hero to his younger brothers. He's a Naval flight officer and graduate of the U.S. Naval Academy. Soon after flying out to see Ian in the hospital, Wes wrote this on our CaringBridge website:

> Hey, Ian, I'm writing this because I think everyone who reads this should know how incredibly tough you are. As I've had the privilege of being with you for the past couple of days, I've been floored by the grace and resolve with which you deal with the pain and discomfort you're in. It humbles me. I had a moment of clarity the first day I was there as to why Lance Armstrong got so much better at bike racing after cancer. After fighting like you are through so much seemingly unending pain, the world's most grueling competition must have paled in comparison. I have always heard people say, "You are my hero," to people going through cancer or things like it, and I have always thought that was kinda odd. I still think it's a little odd, but as I have watched you these past few days, I can really say that I am in awe of you, and you are my hero.

You can imagine the impact that had on all of us.

As chemotherapy took its toll, late one night I woke up in the ICU to find Ian sitting up in bed, literally tearing out his hair. He was crying as he pulled it out in clumps. It's uncomfortable to sleep in piles of hair.

But more importantly, this was one of those defining moments when you hold in your hand the evidence of what you wish was not real. Wes so identified with Ian that the next day he called and asked if we could get on a webcam together. We did, and we laughed our hearts out as Wes and a friend shaved their heads in solidarity with Ian.

But inside, Wes was struggling with doubts. He struggled with how this whole prayer thing works on the rock face of reality. One night he called me as he was on his way to a house-church meeting. They would be discussing prayer, especially what it means to pray without doubting in circumstances like those we were facing.

Throughout Ian's illness I prayed for healing with many godly people. I've had an up close and personal look at how people view prayer and healing and doubt. I observed them carefully, because Ian's illness was taking us down paths I'd never walked before, asking familiar questions with fresh urgency.

As Wes and I talked, it occurred to me that when we struggle with doubts, we need to think carefully about what we doubt. There are some things we must never doubt. I wrote some of them down that night:

- We must never doubt God or God's goodness. That is at the root of the original sin — doubting that God really has our best interests in mind, wondering if He is holding out on us. It would be easy to doubt God's goodness now. But I've seen far too much of God's goodness to doubt it. That would be like doubting that water is wet while I'm swimming in the ocean. No, I don't doubt God's goodness, even now.

- We must never doubt whether God does miracles today. Many believers subtly doubt this, and I'm sure that God is not pleased. I think this may be the most common kind of doubt among God's people today. They'd never say it. They'd never even allow that thought to fully form in their minds. But to many, the idea that God would instantly and dramatically heal Ian overnight is inconsistent with their gut-level experience and thinking about how God works today. This is similar to the heart attitude that restrained Jesus from doing many miracles in Nazareth.

• We must never doubt what God has clearly said. This also is at the root of the original sin. The serpent said, "Has God said . . . ?" (Genesis 3:1, NASB). This kind of doubt is why God struck Zechariah mute when he didn't believe his wife, Elizabeth, could be pregnant (Luke 1:18-20). If God says it, we must not doubt it.

Yet this is where it can get confusing for us mere mortals. This tests our exegesis of the words of God ("What does that passage really mean?"). This tries our acuity in recognizing the voice of God ("What is God really saying to me now?").

I believe that those who walk with God and develop the consistent habit of obeying everything He asks of them do cultivate a well-tuned, subjective sensitivity to God's voice. And I believe that God is much more inclined to speak in special ways to those who consistently trust and obey Him. I also believe that some become cavalier in carelessly asserting specific things that they think God has said, or want God to have said. They stoned Old Testament prophets for such things.

So where does that leave us in our praying? How can we pray with confidence while submitting to God's absolute sovereignty in our lives? I feel like a child boldly asking my good heavenly Father for what I want, while trusting Him to sort out what is best. My kids do this with me. "Can I have more dessert?" "Can I have the keys to your car?" They're not shy about asking. They don't always like my answers. But I hope that in the long run they are deeply convinced that I have their best interests in mind.

When we are pressed to the ragged edge of faith, our doubts are flushed out into the open. And we must deal with them honestly. That is part of the gift of pain.

WARRIORS AND CHILDREN

One day one of our pastors laid his big, weathered hands on Ian's head and said, "Look into my eyes, young man. Yes, I see it! As I've been sitting here watching you, I see in you a warrior spirit." Remarkably, throughout the next twenty-four hours, several other people offered the same affirmation of Ian. The term *warrior* kept coming up unprompted—a strange term to describe a twelve-year-old in bed! Jesus was speaking truth and hope and courage into my son.

This same pastor told us that he believed God healed him of cancer primarily through the prayers of children. Their faith is so pure and undiluted. He urged us to recruit children to pray for Ian, and we did. Oh, how God loves the faith of children! And He does not hold back from conscripting them as child soldiers on the front lines of faith.

Linda has the same instincts about the prayers of children.

When I first got cancer, many people prayed for my healing. But to be honest, what I really wanted was children praying for me. I didn't believe I'd die, but if others believed it, they wouldn't be able to pray with conviction. I wanted effective prayers, so this what I told people: "I don't want you hoping I'll be okay; I want you believing God can and will heal me. Children can lift up the most believing prayers with a faith that is purer, untainted by the lifelong knowledge that things often don't work out as we hope."

The day my diagnosis was announced at church, women sobbed when they tried to talk to me, men spoke with sympathetic concern, and everyone said how sorry they were. One blessed woman boldly said, "Well, Linda, I'm sure if anyone can handle it, you can."

It was like a "pre-funeral." I went there feeling fine and upbeat but came home feeling as though everyone expected me to be dead within a week. It was pretty depressing. I knew they were dealing with their own emotions, but they so clearly did not expect me to survive. Stage IIIC clear-cell ovarian cancer has few survivors.

Adults know this; kids don't. Kids started to pray for me that day in Sunday school class, innocently doing what they knew they were supposed to do, without prejudging what God could handle. No wonder I wanted their prayers!

I don't greet bad news with drama because I want others to see hope in my response. I want them to know I'll lift up my prayers with childlike hope and expectation, not fear.

> But when he asks, he must believe and not doubt, because he who doubts is like a wave of the sea, blown and tossed by the wind. That man should not think he will receive anything from the Lord; he is a double-minded man, unstable in all he does. (James 1:6-8, NIV)

If I ask with doubt in my innermost being, then I might as well not ask. Childlike faith is beautiful, and it's a shame we lose it. One of my greatest joys is being able to recapture that faith. Even though we've grown up and now live in predictable reality, sometimes we need to suspend disbelief and expect the impossible.

Of course, the prayers of children do not guarantee that God will do what we want. In fact, in a later chapter we'll see how much we have to learn from how children respond when God says no. But after walking with Him for thirty years, I'm still learning the depth of what Jesus meant when He pointed to the faith of children as our model. Sometimes our own children are our best teachers.

Linda remembers her and her children's youthful need for comfort when scared or hurt, in light of Ian's amazing calm.

October 15, 2008

I was eight years old, waiting for my parents to get me from my first week of sleepover camp. After a great week of stretching my timid ways, I was excited at the thought of seeing Mom and Dad again. The moment they appeared over the top of the hill, I lost it. Suddenly unable to swallow, I ran as fast as I could, hugged Dad, and burst into tears.

When my own kids were little, they'd get hurt but bravely not cry—until they saw me. Their tears flowed as I enclosed them in my arms. It wasn't so much their hurt as the comfort of Mom's arms. Kids can be brave only so long. Part of our job as parents is to provide a comfortable safe haven, right? But what if there is no safe place?

When Ian was diagnosed with little chance of survival, I asked, "Where's the comfort in that?"

One afternoon when I was visiting Ian, something beeped and he cried out. The room suddenly filled with nurses and machines. In a tense moment, Renee rushed to stand at his feet, I stood out of the way, and Dave held his hand while the nurses quickly tended to him.

Ian, still in pain, called out, "Mom! Lean over quickly! Put your head by my feet!" "What's wrong?" she gasped, lowering her head. He smiled and wiggled his toes. "I just wanted to make you smell my feet." He laughed. After a stunned moment of silence, we all laughed in relief, the tension broken. I think she called him a little creep.

Recently, he had another difficult period. He'd just finished thirty-five hours of chemo in five days. I called Renee, but Ian answered. Trying to offer some comfort, I said, "I hear you just had a pretty rough week." He answered simply, "Yeah, well, it's over now. Want to talk to Mom?" With no self-pity, no complaints, he was ready to move on. I was speechless. Ian had casually reminded me of what I already knew. No matter what we do or say, it's all in God's hands.

Linda's son Sam is several years older than Ian but has Asperger's syndrome, a mild form of autism that affects emotions rather than intelligence. When Ian was diagnosed, Linda watched for signs that Sam might need assurance on the state of her own health. One day she wrote of how Sam shows the same kind of trust that we saw in Ian.

November 15, 2008

Sam and Linda

Last night Sam and I discussed the concept of worry. He'd never tell me how he feels; autistic people don't "do" feelings. I decided to ask him if my health and cancer ever worry him. He said he sees no point in worrying. He's impatient, and he gets angry over things not happening, but he's right. I've never really known him to worry. He doesn't seem to "get" the concept of worry. It's too abstract. He thinks in absolutes. I told him it was actually biblical to not worry. He explained to me, "There's no point in worrying over your health, Mom. It is what it is, so we pray and leave it up to God." Profound thoughts from someone who has such handicaps in this life, but God has given him ways to cope that sometimes are beyond what a "normal" person can handle.

JUST CURIOUS

God is willing to go to great lengths to cultivate faith, even in children. In fact, He calls all of us back to childlike faith: "Truly I say to you, whoever does not receive the kingdom of God like a child will not enter it at all" (Mark 10:15, NASB).

One day, after Ian had been bleeding internally and in horrible pain for a week, I found myself at the end of my own strength and consciously took the posture of a child:

Loving Father, I have a question. I'm not insisting that You answer it immediately, but at some point I'd really like to know why You are keeping us waiting for Ian's healing. I'm not complaining. Really! I know You are working on his behalf. I have no doubt that You are variously lying in bed beside him, hovering over him, touching him tenderly, and continually stationing spirit warriors at his side. And You've mobilized hundreds and hundreds of people all over the world to earnestly pray.

Yet so far it seems like things are getting worse. What's that all about? Is it like in a war movie when the commander holds his forces in check until the last possible moment so that his attack has the maximum effect on the enemy? Is this a dramatic pause so that You will have our full attention? Or is this a longer story, a story where Your glory is revealed in less dramatic ways along a difficult path? Whatever You have in mind, I'm eager for everyone to see You as You really are: glorious.

You don't owe me an answer. I trust You with this. I'm just curious, Lord.

Before all this, there had been more than a few days when I had secretly been troubled by the hardness of my own heart. At times, I had become bored with life and ministry. At other times, I had drifted into self-righteous stagnation. I often had trouble gathering the resolve to do the right things. At times, I fell down miserably. And I longed for the days of fresh new faith and exciting, desperate dependence on God. I recalled the days when I just did whatever God seemed to say, as if I didn't know any better. I longed for the days when I hadn't yet learned that the average Christian lives in quiet, restrained disappointment and desperation. And occasionally I prayed for renewal, a return to childlike faith.

Then God broke through in the most painful ways. He pushed me out into the deep water to restore my desperate yet peaceful dependence on Him.

I am so grateful.

SUNDANCE'S LEAP OF FAITH

I wish this were automatic. I wish each of us came with standard factory equipment that guaranteed we would trust God no matter what, at every moment, in every circumstance. Or do I? I guess that would make us robots. Do I want a lover or a slave girl as my wife? I want a wife who *chooses* to love me with all of her heart and chooses to trust me in spite of my failures. Fortunately, we have a Lover who has never failed to love us and never will. Yet we still struggle with trusting Him completely. And He leaves the choice to us. He does not force it. But He sure gives us opportunities to trust Him—or not.

Pain pushes us to make a choice. People are right when they say that difficulties can make us either bitter or better. We can choose to give up and collapse into hopelessness. It can feel like we don't have any reasonable choice at all, like being offered a choice between dying by firing squad or by guillotine. But actually we're being offered a choice as to how we'll live rather than how we'll die. And it remains a choice for which we are responsible. Consider what Linda wrote in her church newsletter seven years into her battle with cancer:

There's a scene in the movie *Butch Cassidy and the Sundance Kid* that's classic. Butch and Sundance are being pursued by officer Woodcock. They're at the edge of a cliff with no way out, Woodcock and his men closing in on them. Butch frantically screams to Sundance to jump into the river far below so they can get away. Sundance refuses, finally blurting out, "I can't swim!" It's funny but ironic, since Sundance is seemingly a hardened outlaw with no fear of anyone or anything.

A few years ago, I had to make the same leap Sundance eventually made, in faith—off a cliff, into the unknown, with no possible way of saving myself. In Acts 14, Paul told a crippled man, "Stand up on your feet!" (verse 10, NIV), and in faith, the man jumped up and walked. Did I have that kind of faith?

People often tell me that they admire my great faith in the midst of cancer, as though it were something I've done on my own. I do have deep faith, but it didn't originate within me. Like Sundance, I just gave up on my own ability to save myself where I was and "jumped" into God's arms, having no idea what His plan was for me. With no other choice, I simply trusted Him to catch me.

My faith is a gift that sees me through this adventure. Don't admire me; thank God for His great mercy, for giving people like me a hope that's real and gives peace. It's in that hope that Steve and I rest and take whatever comes along.

Listen, folks, do you have faith in Jesus? Well, therein lies your ability to be healed of your afflictions. The choice of healing—whether of physical, emotional, or any other pain—is God's. Just stop trying to save yourself, stop hunting for another way out, stop relying on man's abilities, and jump off that cliff. Once you're no longer trying to do it on your own, you'll see where He takes you. It's the safest place you can be. I couldn't feel safer.

I'M JUST LIKE YOU

Let's not pretend this is easy. And let's not pretend that anyone resolves this issue once and for all. Linda has stood on the edge of one cliff after another through her years of cancer. Recently, she wrote this as she peered over the edge again:

I like my oncology nurses, but frankly, I prefer to never see them again. It's not that they're ugly, mean, and inflict pain (well, there was a bit of that, but Elaine always said she was sorry). It was all those smells, tubes, blood, and poison. Not to mention pounding bone pain, utter weariness, hair loss, blistered feet, and bloating caused by steroids.

Yes, I'm used to it. Yes, I've known for seven and a half years this would be a recurring fact of life as long as I live. Yes, every day my life expectancy is unknown. (Wait, so is yours.) Yes, I can write with humor and a carefree attitude about it all. But just so you know, I hate this. Big surprise. Don't think I have some unusual capacity to cope with this that enables me to keep going with humor and resolve. I don't. I'm just like you. **I'm just like you.**

I want you to know that alone, in my own head and heart, I often feel broken and tired and angry about the whole stinkin' thing. But God has always stepped in exactly when I need Him. It's like He can read my mind or something. Oh, right.

Are you miserable? Do you think you can't be brave, that you can't stand another day of heartache, that you could never handle cancer as I do, that you hate your life and wonder why God is so very far away? Or are you hurting from your wife ignoring you, your husband snapping at you, your kids being brats, your parents demanding too much, your job being at risk, or no money to pay bills?

Whatever your pain, it's no less than mine. If you hurt, you hurt. Cancer only sounds worse since it can be so public — and so life-ending. It scares people. But trust me, it's definitely not the worst I've had to endure. That "capacity to cope" I mentioned isn't mine. It's God's grace. Please don't think I have something you don't (except for cancer, of course). All it takes is a willingness to believe, submit, and know you can't handle it alone.

Want to grow a tomato without God? Good luck. You can decide to plant the seed in the earth and nurture it, but God does the growing. Want to rest in the midst of heartache? Good luck. But decide to give the pain to God, and He'll grow peace in you. You simply cannot do it alone.

Jairus, the synagogue ruler, came to Jesus, asking Him to heal his sick daughter. While on their way to her, they heard she'd died. Jesus told him, "Don't be afraid; just believe" (Mark 5:36, NIV). Yeah, right; his daughter's already dead; just what was he supposed to believe? But he continued to trust and follow Jesus home, still believing in an impossible conclusion. If Jairus had said, "Forget it; she's already dead; You can't do anything now," it would have been over.

If God seems far away, go to Him and ask. Doesn't it make sense that if Jesus could raise this child, He could get you through whatever you're suffering if you'd just ask Him in faith? What impossible thing are you willing to believe God can handle?

Don't be afraid. Just believe.

ROLLER COASTERS AND "WHAT IFS"

I have always been one to seek faith adventures. I love the thrill when God calls us to trust Him for an impossible amount of money or calls us into a ministry opportunity that will surely fail unless He comes through. But my wife, though a profound encourager of my faith, prefers to avoid the high cliffs of faith. And honestly, even I would prefer to choose when and how my faith is tested. But that's not the way it works.

Wise friends warned us that living with cancer would be like a roller coaster, with dramatic ups and downs. Renee avoids roller coasters like most of us avoid the flu. She has always gladly stayed behind with the little ones while I take our teenagers on the biggest, baddest rides we can find. I love (and hate) that moment when we are approaching the crest and the coaster is slowly clack, clack, clacking just before we plunge into oblivion, screaming our heads off. Not Renee. She's happier to keep her feet quietly on firm ground. So this note she wrote as we crested one of our cancer turns is especially poignant. It captures the way God wants us to live.

Today feels like one of the down slopes of the roller coaster—waiting to hear results from the latest CT scan. God has not given us a spirit of fear, but of power, and love, and a sound mind. Okay, but my stomach still does its flip-flops as I struggle with "what if." I am churning as I cling to Him, trusting and waiting to hear what the pictures tell us of what is happening inside my son. What if? No matter what, I WILL trust in the King of Glory. The fear is not from Him. He is my Shepherd; He promised to lead me beside quiet waters. So we wait, and we bow down, and we surround ourselves with praise of our King.

Sometimes God calls our bluff. Renee's "what if" became our reality on April 27, 2009, when Ian left us and joined that great cloud of witnesses in heaven. What we had most feared came upon us with force.

By the next night all of our children had arrived home, and we sat around the dinner table until nearly midnight. We have a family tradition of giving gifts of affirmation to celebrate a birthday. So we did that with Ian, sharing our favorite memories and deep feelings. Tears flowed freely, and laughter shook the walls of the very room in which we had cared for Ian.

We also began to wrestle with the hard questions. I am so proud of how my children refuse to dodge the hard questions and will not accept trite answers. In view of the torrents of bold faith displayed by us and so many others, why have we seen God heal others but not Ian? That night and still today we are disoriented but steadfast in trusting God Himself. That's the mystery, even to us.

As Ian was leaving his body, I was silently praying from the core of my being, *God, I trust You, I love You, I praise You.* And Renee turned to me and said with firm resolve, "We will continue to trust." We had walked with God deeply for decades, and we had come to know Him too well to throw all that aside in the face of this.

There were (and are) many unanswered questions. A wise friend urged me to give those questions time. They are like wine that needs time to ferment and mature before opening. I told my children how the Enemy loves to take advantage of the experience of trauma to plant lies deep in our souls, lies that are rooted in emotionally distorted perceptions of God and life. For some, it is the trauma of sexual or emotional abuse. For others, it is violence or war. For others, it is divorce or betrayal. Regardless of the trauma, the Enemy is quick to whisper lies. And in the heat of the moment, we are tempted to take those lies into the depths of our souls: "I'll never trust like that again. I'll never love like that again. God doesn't care." Those lies enslave us and can destroy us. Big questions are best addressed after the waves of emotion have settled, and we're not there yet.

Such is life on the ragged edge of faith. As for us, we will continue to trust.

QUESTIONS FOR REFLECTION

- ▶ What do you think of this statement, "Pain is always an invitation to something you cannot see at the moment"?
- ▶ Has the Enemy used your pain to plant lies in your soul? What are those lies?
- ▶ As heaven's cloud of witnesses watches your faith these days, what might they find encouraging?

CHAPTER 5

A Thin Place

A few days after Ian was first admitted to intensive care, nine of us gathered around his bed. As we sang of God's glory and the Father's love, some knelt, some laid hands on Ian, and tears flowed among us all. At one point a nurse peeked in and realized it was a holy moment. It was one of those "thin places" where the space between us and heaven becomes translucent, when God pulls back the veil and allows us to see.

Writer Michael Mullen described the thin places this way:

> On this arid summit, where the winds blow hard, where no root takes hold, where distance seems infinite and heaven close, the spirit is tested and replenished . . . for the pilgrim has reached a thin place, where one steps into the highest dimension of one's existence.[1]

We love these moments, but we prefer to seek them on our terms: during a moving time of worship, at a retreat when the fog of daily life recedes, as we watch a beautiful sunset. Sometimes God ushers us into thin places we never sought. Often, pain is the vestibule.

LOVE CAME TO TOWN

In the person of Jesus, the barrier between heaven and earth disappeared. Jesus told everyone who would listen that in Him, the kingdom of God had come to town. I think that's what it was like when Jesus came to Galilee:

> "The people living in darkness
> have seen a great light;
> on those living in the land of the shadow of death
> a light has dawned."
>
> From that time on Jesus began to preach, *"Repent, for the kingdom of heaven is near."* (Matthew 4:16-17, NIV, emphasis added)

Jesus wanted everyone to see what it was like where He'd come from. He wanted everyone to experience the beauty He had known and still knew. Before I saw Yosemite Falls in California, the most beautiful place I'd ever seen was Colorado's Garden of the Gods and Glen Eyrie, where I now work. When others mention a trip to Colorado Springs, I eagerly ask, "Have you seen Glen Eyrie?" I want them to experience it too. I think it was like that for Jesus. I'm sure He wanted others to see what He saw and to experience what He experienced. He was willing to go to great lengths to help them see.

Unfortunately, we are normally blinded by the mundane things that surround us. We can't see the stars until it's dark.

I believe part of why Jesus sought out people in pain was because they were most sensitive to His message. Soon they were seeking Him. Wherever He went, the sick thronged to see Him, to touch Him and be touched. And Jesus enlisted and empowered His disciples to join Him in revealing the kingdom to those in pain, telling them to heal the sick and affirm that "the kingdom of God has come near to you."

I long to live among people in such a way that it is apparent the kingdom of God has come near. Sometimes I do live that way. And as with Jesus and His disciples, those thin places often come in the midst of pain. But the revealing comes only for those who have ears to hear and eyes to see: "Truly, truly, I say to you, unless one is born again [literally, 'born from above'] *he cannot see the kingdom of God*" (John 3:3, NASB, emphasis added).

In the midst of pain, it is God's Spirit that leads us into thin places. He brings us to an intersection of two worlds, where the seen and the unseen overlap in mysterious ways. We are given glimpses of the kingdom breaking through here on earth, just as Jesus said.

"I KNOW BETTER"

It's easier to see the kingdom of God from the mountaintops, or even the valleys. But these aren't the places we normally live. Lessons learned in the high and low places should transform how we see everyday life in the plains, where the kingdom of God is still near.

A few months after Ian's initial diagnosis, he prayed that he would be healthy enough to join his friends at a big youth conference. He wanted to go back to just being a kid. He longed to return to life on the plains. God enabled him to go to the conference, but it was apparent that he was no longer the same boy. Although he could still be incredibly irritating at times—and fought with his brothers every day—those thin places had changed him somehow.

After the conference Ian said to his mom, "Some people say that miracles don't happen today. Yeah, right. Mom, I know better!" Renee laughed with joy to see her son *know* he was living God's miracle. His words? "I've grown closer to God." Indeed he had.

I thought back to my prayer that first night in the hospital, asking God that somehow through the pain Ian would come to know Him as He really is. Although I wished God had used some other method, the deepest desire of my heart for Ian was coming to life. While other boys were wondering about the whole God thing, the miraculous nearness of God's kingdom was now obvious to Ian.

I remember when I began to recognize God's loving presence in my everyday life. It was an otherwise mundane moment in a mundane day. But thirty years later it is preserved in my memory as a freeze-frame moment. I remember the corner where I was turning into the local mall. It was raining, and I was impatient with the traffic. But as I waited, a little boy in the car in front of me wiped the fog from the rear window of the car, and through the raindrops coursing down the window he caught my eye, smiled, and waved. It was that simple. But somehow in that moment my eyes were opened to see that God Himself was smiling at me through that boy. The sovereign grace of God had morphed from a theological theory to a personal truth. God had broken through in that thin place, and He changed the way I see the world.

Before that day I might have just felt lucky.

LUCKY?

Luck is an idea that can blind us to God's providence and to the thin places in everyday life. Sometimes God's providence shines through in the small things of everyday life, even through a smiling little boy. At other times God shows Himself so clearly that luck seems too empty and inadequate an explanation. Less than a month into Ian's illness, we were wrestling with our part in caring for him when we got really "lucky."

From David's Journal
March 1, 2008

There "just happened" to be a Christian physicians conference here in Colorado Springs this weekend. Our dear friend Rick, a doctor from Oklahoma, "coincidentally" was here for the conference and heard about Ian. He immediately arranged to come pray with us.

Just before coming, "by chance" he mentioned Ian's situation to Jairo, a new acquaintance in his small group at the conference. Jairo "happens" to be one of the best oncologists in the country. He is a protégé of the man who won the Nobel Peace Prize for his work on bone marrow transplants. Rick was surprised to realize that Jairo is doing cutting-edge research on the very form of cancer Ian has. Remember, only about fifty people a year get this disease.

Rick arranged for us to have lunch with Jairo, and we described Ian's progress to him. From his experience with alveolar rhabdomyo-sarcoma, he described Ian's progress as miraculous.

It became clear that this doctor's passion is treating cancer through nutrition. You may remember that, "coincidentally," nutrition is also Renee's passion. After he quickly walked us through a blizzard of technical medical details, he recommended an unusual supplement to help Ian rebuild his immune system. It "just so happened" that a friend had purchased that very supplement for us as a gift, and it was already sitting on our counter at home.

I guess we're just lucky.

Actually, I don't know what luck is, and I sure don't put my faith in it. But here's what I do know: "In all things God works for the good of those who love him, who have been called according to his purpose" (Romans 8:28, NIV). I hasten to say that this would be true even if things did not seem to be improving. But right now it is easy for us to see the fingerprints of the Blessed Controller of All Things.

Today Ian was sighted walking around the block, swamped by neighborhood kids coming to see him, playing at a neighbor's house, and going to a movie with his friends. This is the same kid who before today had not walked from the guest room to the couch without assistance. Was that luck, or a glimpse of God at work?

This note from Linda illustrates how she has rejected the idea of luck as well:

Long before cancer threatened to take my life, I should have died one morning on my way to do some shopping. I guess I was lucky. My dictionary says *luck* is "an unknown or unpredictable phenomenon that causes an event to result one way rather than another." Some call it luck; some of us call it God's grace.

Something urged me to pray for travel safety before I left home that morning, which seemed odd since I had no plans to go more than three miles from home. I prayed anyway. Why not?

I drove alone to the four-lane intersection near our home. First in line at the light, I did what many people do while waiting for the light to change—I watched for a hint of yellow on the intersecting light so I'd be ready to shift my manual transmission into first gear and go when my light turned green.

Seeing the yellow on the light's rim, I put my hand on the stick shift and tried to shift the gear. Nothing happened. It wasn't that the stick wouldn't move; it was that my hand wouldn't move. I actually looked at my own hand in amazement, wondering, What on earth? Horns began to honk. I tried with all my might to make my hand move, but it was as though I had no control over my own hand. It just sat there, limp, as I stared at it. My heart started to race as I realized that people were beginning to get angry with me, but I couldn't do anything. No one behind me could move, and I was apparently paralyzed.

Keep in mind that this all took place in about four seconds, but you know some people won't wait half a second for traffic to move, so I was taking eight times too long. As thoughts sped through my frantic mind as to what on earth was wrong with my disobedient hand, I looked up just as an out-of-control car sped through the intersection from my left without stopping or slowing down, right through the place I'd have been if I had pulled out when I tried to.

My chest hurt from my pounding heart. The honking behind me stopped as others also saw what we all had avoided. I could see the shock on other people's faces. My hand finally started to move again according to my brain's commands, so I pulled out, only to pull over again as soon as I could. I thanked God for coming into my car, holding my hand, and saving my life. That thin place between heaven and my Chevy Cavalier had come upon me in a very real way.

To this day, I'm still awed when I recall that moment. More than twenty years later I still remember feeling the very real presence of the Holy Spirit. I know He isn't going to let me miss any of what He has planned for me. He knew back then that I was eventually going to live through a decade (or more) with cancer, and He's still here holding my hand today.

How fortunate! Fate smiled on her. Some people just live a charmed life. Really? Those innocent little sayings blind us to something much greater and more amazing than the vague notion of luck. Those who are not blinded by the idea of luck can peer through thin places every day.

THE MASTER OF BREAKTHROUGH

Some people seem to have a clearer view into those thin places — perhaps because they are more aware of their own desperation. In 2 Samuel 5, the Philistines were becoming alarmed about David's rise to power, so they turned out in force to attack him. It's easy for us to read such Old Testament stories with cool indifference and to lose sight of the ugly realities of hand-to-hand combat. We see war through the filters of CNN. But David and his men had dragged too many bloody corpses from the battlefield to view the Philistine army as simply characters in a video game. They were in real danger; adrenaline was pumping hard.

Then David inquired of the LORD, saying, "Shall I go up against the Philistines? Will You give them into my hand?" And the LORD said to David, "Go up, for I will certainly give the Philistines into your hand." So David came to Baal-perazim and defeated them there; and he said, "The LORD has broken through my enemies before me like the breakthrough of waters." Therefore he named that place Baal-perazim. (verses 19-20, NASB)

We used to have an old blue station wagon with the license plate "BLPRZM." We would explain to puzzled inquirers that BLPRZM stood for Baal-perazim, Hebrew for "The Master of Breakthrough." We would go on to explain the way that God had broken through to provide that old car when we had nowhere else to turn. I don't know what others thought, but whenever our children heard us tell that story, it reinforced in their hearts that when you are cornered like King David, or like Mom and Dad without a car, you should look for God to break through into your world and come to your rescue. It's not easy to get to know God that way. A breakthrough from heaven often comes as a result of pain and desperation.

GOD SIGHTINGS

Often at our dinner table Renee will ask, "Did anyone have a God sighting today?" She's trolling for "glory stories," her response to the warning in Romans 1:

For since the creation of the world God's invisible qualities— his eternal power and divine nature—have been clearly seen, being understood from what has been made, so that men are without excuse.

For although they knew God, they neither glorified him as God nor gave thanks to him, but their thinking became futile and their foolish hearts were darkened. (verses 20-21, NIV)

She's cultivating in us a way of seeing God's glory in everyday life. It is there for all to see, but we can fail to recognize it or to give thanks.

And that lays foundations for becoming futile and dark in our thinking. Seasons of pain are particularly ripe for both approaches. We can get ticked off with God and lose sight of His kindnesses along the way, or we can see glimpses of God all around us. Here's how this played out for Renee as we walked through chemotherapy with Ian:

From Renee's Journal
August 28, 2008

David is in Kenya, and we are in normal, productive chaos here in the Lyons' Den. I regularly ask each one in my family for their "God sighting" for the day. As we see God and then praise Him in the midst of our "dailies," we begin to think His thoughts after Him. The majesty of the mountains out my kitchen window, snuggled up against the sweeping, brilliant blue sky, is often what helps me keep the tumult of each day focused on the Sustainer of all I see.

We are back into the struggles of chemotherapy with all the uglies that are folded into that package. I had asked God if He would be willing to continue with miracles in these coming months since He seems to be enjoying touching Ian with His lavishness so far. I asked if He would keep Ian's red blood count above 9 so that he would not have to have any more transfusions. My God sighting for today: We got his count back, and his red blood count is 10.5. That is great for someone on extended chemo. Unfortunately, he has no white blood count, so we are into "isolation" as much as we can for a kid who feels great other than being extra tired. And he is in danger of bleeding because of almost no platelets. I'm trying to keep him off his bike and scooter, and ask him to please stop wrestling out in the yard! I praise my Father for answering this mother's plea for that one more thing this week.

Meanwhile, back east Linda was having her own God sightings.

> Some days I am sick, sick, sick of talking about having cancer. I just want people to shut up about it. I want it to end. Then one day a customer comes into the shop late, and as a result I have to work late, and I'm sick from a cold, anxious to get home, and don't care about selling one more thing. Then the customer sees the picture of Ian, which leads to a talk about cancer and faith. And as she leaves, she turns and says, "I didn't even want or plan to come here today, but when I drove by, something told me I had to turn back. And now I realize why. I'm renewed in my own faith by listening to you. Your family is amazing. Your faith is amazing. I pray that I will not have to bear the burdens that you all have, but I appreciate that God uses you to encourage me how to live my life from what He's taught you. Through you, He has given me a gift."
>
> Um, and I wanted her to leave so I could go home?

God sightings are so easy to miss, but so precious when we have eyes to see that the kingdom of God really has drawn near.

ENCOUNTERS WITH THE AUTHOR

Each of us is caught up in a story much greater than ourselves. Our story is in the nonfiction section, where real people are being pursued by a real God in the mother of all love stories. In thin places, we get to transcend the pages and actually encounter the Author. Cancer has ushered us into many such encounters, one of which was particularly memorable:

From David's Journal
February 22, 2008

Today, as Nancy Gallegos played the harp beside Ian's bed, nurses brought children from other rooms to listen at the door. Nancy and her husband, Dennis, are invited into hospitals in the area to play and pray for the sick. They are humble, gentle, winsome, and full of faith. While Nancy played,

Dennis and Nancy Gallegos and their harp

we knelt around Ian's bed and poured out our hearts to God. It was another one of those "thin places" where the boundary between heaven and earth is blurred.

After about a half hour, I had a recurring, invasive thought, one of those thoughts that I know was not my own. "Read Psalm 18. READ PSALM 18!" After the third or fourth prompting (I can be slow), I went to find my Bible. It's a very dramatic psalm of David celebrating how God delivered him from his troubles. I felt led to read the whole psalm out loud to Ian as Nancy played. As I did, Dennis lurched from his chair to my side to show me that God had him reading the very same psalm! I read with a great sense that God was speaking to Ian, and to us.

> In my distress I called to the LORD;
>   I cried to my God for help.
> From his temple he heard my voice;
>   my cry came before him, into his ears.
> The earth trembled and quaked,
>   and the foundations of the mountains shook;
>   they trembled because he was angry. . . .
>   He rescued me because he delighted in me. . . .
>   He shows unfailing kindness to his anointed,
>   to David and his descendants forever. (verses 6-7,19,50, NIV)

In my mind, I saw God rising from His throne to rush to save His anointed one. I felt the earth shaking at His approach, as He comes to rescue one in whom He delights. One like Ian.

Would we have had such encounters with the Author without all the pain we've known? Perhaps. But God seems to use pain, sometimes sustained pain, to chip away the ice on our windshield so that we can see. Once when I was wondering why God kept us waiting for Ian to be healed, Linda wrote this to me:

> If God had healed me right away, I would have missed so much. Well, so much pain, yes, but so much of His blessings, too. I learned things through that initial time of suffering that I doubt I would have learned any other way, and God knew that. It's a steep price to pay for knowledge, but it's knowledge that's invaluable to me, knowledge that led me to a relationship with God that is amazing.

When the Make-A-Wish Foundation offered Ian a wish, one of his top three choices was to meet Brian Jacques, the author of his favorite fantasy series. I puzzled over why a thirteen-year-old boy would want to "waste" his wish on that when he could go on a real adventure instead. Now I think I may understand. Ian had so entered into those stories that meeting the author would be like meeting the creator of another world.

Ironically, Ian's own story allowed us a meeting with the greatest Author we could ever know.

KNOWING GOD AS HE REALLY IS

Do you really want to meet the Author? Are you sure? Do you want to encounter God as He is? Or as you wish Him to be? If we're honest, most of us are not sure we want to encounter God as He really is. We'd much rather play with a god who is tame and plays by our rules. We're not alone in that desire. Soon after leaving Egypt, the Israelites ran into a thin place that was a little too close for comfort:

> When the people saw the thunder and lightning and heard the trumpet and saw the mountain in smoke, they trembled with fear. They stayed at a distance and said to Moses, "Speak to us yourself and we will listen. But do not have God speak to us or we will die."
>
> Moses said to the people, "Do not be afraid. God has come to test you, so that the fear of God will be with you to keep you from sinning."
>
> The people remained at a distance, while Moses approached the thick darkness where God was. (Exodus 20:18-21, NIV)

Like Israel, most of us want to know God, but on our own terms. Only a few, like Moses, will risk walking into the darkness where God lives. And then there are some of us who innocently and earnestly pray wild prayers about wanting to know God "whatever it takes." God listens and escorts us into the darkness Himself. He takes us to places we would never want to go so that there we can encounter Him.

Maybe Moses had heard the story of Job, the oldest story in the Bible. Job was one of those who prayed wild prayers out of his deep longing to walk closely with God.

> When the days of feasting had completed their cycle, Job would send and consecrate [his children], rising up early in the morning and offering burnt offerings according to the number of them all; for Job said, "Perhaps my sons have sinned and cursed God in their hearts." Thus Job did continually. (Job 1:5, NASB)

This regular consecration, this frequent relinquishing of ownership, prepared Job for the tragedies that came his way. Job had continually reminded himself that his children belonged to God. So he could say, "The LORD gave and the LORD has taken away. Blessed be the name of the LORD" (1:21, NASB). He could say, "Shall we indeed accept good from God and not accept adversity?" (2:10, NASB).

Job's daily consecration of his children did not protect them from adversity or tragedy. But it did protect Job's heart. Although Job struggled deeply with his tragedies, his heart had been prepared. He held his children and all that he owned with open hands. Job may not have fully realized that he had a vicious and sadistic enemy. But God had Job's enemy on a leash. Ultimately, Job came to realize this: Before tragedy struck, he had merely heard about God. But because his heart had been prepared through tragedy, he came to know God as He really is. And he said, "My ears had heard of you *but now my eyes have seen you*" (Job 42:5, NIV, emphasis added).

And Job knelt in slack-jawed, astonished reverence.

THROUGH THE SHADOWLANDS

Renee and Ian's brother Hudson at Ian's grave

C. S. Lewis was a man acquainted with grief and pain. Late in life he let a young woman named Joy Gresham into his heart, and they were married. Before their marriage had time to fully bloom, Lewis found himself watching his beloved wife die of cancer. The joy and agony of their romance and their walk through the valley of the shadow of death was documented in the movie *Shadowlands*.

We entered into our own shadowlands when Ian died. Here, heaven seems closer, and this world seems dimmer. Worship songs come to life as I imagine Ian singing similar praise before God Himself. I see Ian praying for us now. He is now among those who rejoice over us when we repent and turn back to God (see Luke 15:10).

Learning to see things from the other side, from the perspective Ian now sees, will somehow resolve many questions, making them seem irrelevant or unimportant. From the other side it will be easier to see why God thought it best to heal Ian by taking him to heaven. There, our "Whys?" will become "Wow, now that makes sense!" From there we'll be able to read the last chapter that pulls all things together.

I love the way heaven is described by Quan, the main character in Randy Alcorn's novel *Safely Home*. After Quan dies the seemingly tragic death of a martyr, he arrives in heaven.

Compared to what he now beheld, the world he'd come from was a land of shadows, colorless and two-dimensional. This place was fresh and captivating, resonating with color and beauty. He could not only see and hear it, but feel and smell and taste it. Every hillside, every mountain, every waterfall, every frolicking animal in the fields seemed to beckon him to come join them, to come from the outside and plunge into the inside. This whole world had the feel of cool water on a blistering August afternoon. The light beckoned him to dive in with abandon, to come join the great adventure.

"I know what this is," Quan said.

"Tell me," said the Carpenter.

"It's the substance that casts all those shadows in the other world. The circles there are copies of the spheres here. The squares there are copies of the cubes here. The triangles there are copies of the pyramids here. Earth was a flatland. This is . . . well, the inside is bigger than the outside, isn't it? How many dimensions are there?"

"Far more than you have seen yet," the King said, laughing.

"This is the place that defines and gives meaning to all

places," Li Quan said. "I never imagined it would be like this."[2]

From where Ian lives today, in Paradise, I imagine the questions that trouble us here probably seem strange and out of place. Ian's death brings heaven closer. As the eighteenth-century pastor Benjamin Palmer once said, "Ah! Who can tell how the two worlds may overlap at the border where they touch!"

Thin places give us glimpses of the life for which we were made —and the One for whom we were made. Sometimes we instinctively seek them in worship and nature. Sometimes God chooses to satisfy that longing by dragging us to places where we would never want to go. Either way, if we are willing, we can use the thin places as an opportunity to encounter God as He really is.

QUESTIONS FOR REFLECTION

- ▶ How has your view of God changed in the past twelve months?
- ▶ Complete this statement: "Through pain I am learning that God is my . . ."
- ▶ What "God sightings" have you had recently?

CHAPTER 6

BEAUTY FROM ASHES

We are made for love. We are created to continually receive love and to let it flow through us to others. We are at our best when we live this way. We become radiant, fulfilled, beautiful.

The world tells us that beauty thrives in the absence of pain, when everything is going smoothly. That can be true. But sometimes the truest form of beauty, the kind produced by authentic love, is reserved for life's most painful circumstances. The most beautiful person who ever lived left heaven to wade right into the pain of this world. Look at how He introduced Himself:

> The Spirit of the Lord GOD is upon Me,
> Because the LORD has anointed Me
> To preach good tidings to the poor;
> He has sent Me to heal the brokenhearted,
> To proclaim liberty to the captives,
> And the opening of the prison to those who are bound;
> To proclaim the acceptable year of the LORD,
> And the day of vengeance of our God;
> To comfort all who mourn,
> To console those who mourn in Zion,
> To give them beauty for ashes,

The oil of joy for mourning,
The garment of praise for the spirit of heaviness;
That they may be called trees of righteousness,
The planting of the Lord, that He may be glorified.
            (Isaiah 61:1-3, nkjv)

So beautiful was Jesus' love that it led Him to submit to suffering and death on a cross. (Doesn't it seem strange that today we regard the cross, an instrument of cruel execution, as beautiful?) But then He rose from the dead so that He could come and continue to live through us as His hands, His eyes, His voice—members of His body today.

The other night we were at a sunset concert in the park when, off to the side, one couple quietly rose and began to dance. Soon all eyes were on them, an uninhibited picture of grace and joy. They moved together so beautifully, trusting one another, enjoying one another, expressing their love in such graceful ways. How did they anticipate one another's moves? Practice? Instinct? I don't know. Such things are a beautiful mystery to me—like the mystery of the life and love of Christ flowing through His body.

Unfortunately, that kind of beauty is too rarely expressed among us. It is too often marred beyond recognition by unresolved conflicts, competition, and ungodly attitudes. Those who were designed to live in beautiful harmony digress into ugly dissonance.

There are exceptions, and those exceptions are often birthed in pain. A sick child, a death, a tragic accident suddenly jars us from our self-centered ways, and we find ourselves caring, loving, sacrificing, nurturing, giving—and beauty emerges. Or it should emerge. But it doesn't always work the way God intended. Pain can also flush selfishness and dysfunction out into the open. Too many of us live isolated lives without experiencing the loving relationships that God designed us to experience. Pain can highlight our isolation and make a hard situation even worse.

Linda's friend Susan found herself in that sad place:

Susan and I knew each other through work and our community. After a few years with no contact, she walked into my shop one day and we renewed our acquaintance. I learned that her lovely daughter had married, and Susan was excited about being a new grandmother. She was happy and seemed to have a

Linda's shop where so many heard her story

new lease on life. Her own long marriage had ended, and her new grandson became the focus of much of her love. Whenever Susan stopped by, she glowed when mentioning this little light in her life.

After a while, I noticed she hadn't been in for some time, though she lived nearby. I asked a mutual acquaintance if she knew where Susan was. "You don't know what happened?" I didn't.

A year earlier her grandson had gone to bed one night with a slight fever. Susan's daughter checked on him during the night, deciding to take him to the doctor in the morning. But by morning, they were stunned to find he had died. It was a horrifying time for the whole family. It was no one's fault; no one did anything wrong. A rapidly growing infectious disease cruelly took his young life. I could not imagine the searing pain they all felt. I was instantly filled with sorrow and heartache for my friend, and wrote her a note.

She was devastated, not only in losing her grandson but also over her daughter's own heartbreak. Susan withdrew from people and mourned alone for months, not wanting to talk to or be with anyone. A few days after I sent the note, I heard from her. She seemed genuinely moved by my gesture. She was healing but forever scarred by the loss. Though it had been nearly a year, she was just starting to engage with others again.

I also learned that her daughter and son-in-law had eventually divorced, unable to cope with the heartrending pain and loss they'd suffered. This is not uncommon, and sadly, it's perfectly understandable. When we are weak and hurting, we're most vulnerable to more pain. How I wish someone had reached out to this hurting couple and helped them grieve together, not alone. How I wish I had known, so I could have lifted them up to God for comfort and strength when they couldn't possibly have healed on their own.

At my darkest point, I had no desire, no strength to reach out for help. I wanted to be left alone in my darkened room to cry and hurt. Pain was my only friend. But God knows better, and I thank Him that He never allowed me to be alone again. I don't know all who pray for me, but I do know there are many. Those "pray-ers" carry me through any dark path I encounter. If I ever start to feel alone and abandoned, someone "happens" to call or send me a note of encouragement and prayer, reminding me that we're in this life together.

I am surrounded by people who choose to obey this command: "Carry each other's burdens, and in this way you will fulfill the law of Christ" (Galatians 6:2, NIV). And I've been able to say, "Praise be to the Lord, to God our Savior, who daily bears our burdens" (Psalm 68:19, NIV). You don't think I've survived all this on my own, do you?

I don't know where Susan is spiritually, but what is doubly sad is how many *believers* suffer in isolation, often self-imposed. I guess we feel ashamed of our pain, or we feel a need to protect others from our burdens. In fact, we're often actually protecting ourselves from feeling vulnerable and needy. And then everyone loses. We miss the benefits of being part of the body of Christ. Others miss the opportunity to let Christ's life and love flow through them. And the world around us misses the opportunity to watch the ways that we love one another and see that we really are Jesus' disciples.

Through our pain, Linda and I have experienced love as it should be. We had both endured disappointing relationships with local churches. Then pain invaded our lives, and we chose to share that pain with those around us. It was not an easy choice. We feared rejection or condescending pity, but we were desperate enough to take a risk. And we chose to believe that the Life of Christ would rise within the body of Christ — that others would surrender their temptation to withdraw from us and would instead love us the way Christ Himself loves us. That choice changed everything.

Linda wrote to me:

> It doesn't come naturally for me to let down my guard with others, to admit to or publicize a personal need. I have a fierce independent streak in me. Especially as a woman, I'm on guard against those who still believe women are the inferior half of humanity. I don't like to admit weakness, even though we all feel it at times. But that's pride creeping in. What has changed over the years is my willingness to let down my guard with God and stop pretending He doesn't already know it all anyway. He's completely trustworthy, so it's easier to let go with Him.
>
> As a result, I find my value in Him, not in the opinion others have of me, so I'm more willing to express a weakness. My need is greater than my pride. My confidence in God makes it easier to ask for prayer, knowing that without His intervention, I'm not going to make it through all this. Rather than just being a member of a church, I'm a member of Christ's body, and we're made to need one another. That body includes anyone who lives in Christ, no matter what church they attend.
>
> Recognizing that, it was easy to lay my pain and needs out there for all to see, because it's part of me. The response of others was to feel the pain of this hurting member and act on the urge to pray for me, much like we'd put an ice pack on a hurting arm. When one member is hurting, the body (as it should) feels it and acts on it.

CHURCH, THE WAY IT OUGHT TO BE

When Linda learned that cancer had invaded our lives, she knew all too well the agony that awaited us, but she knew the joys as well. A few weeks into our ordeal, she wrote this to me:

> I remember a dream from seven and a half years ago. I was on my back but moving along, not under my own power but as though weightless. Looking over my shoulder, I could see many, many people. They were underneath me, holding me aloft over their heads, on their uplifted hands and arms. It was almost like a celebration.
>
> They were singing and praising God as they carried me across an empty hill, the same hill where our little church now stands. My feet could not touch the ground; there was no need. I relaxed. They did all the work for me, and I was able to rest, knowing they would never let me fall. When I woke up, I was filled with peace.
>
> It turns out it wasn't a dream after all. The saints who prayed for me were those people who carried me.

One Sunday in the first months of her cancer journey, Linda got to thank the people who had carried her and would not let her fall.

November 2000

> A singer named Clint Black had a hit song with these words: "Love isn't something that we have, it's something that we do." Love is an action verb, and I'm here to say there has been a lot of action in our church this past month.
>
> It has been overwhelming to be the recipients of such an outpouring of love from so many of you, especially since over the past year and a half, Steve and I had come to feel a bit alienated

from the family here. You see, we don't fit the standard evangelical family image when it comes to politics, school choices, trick-or-treating, or the secular music and movies we enjoy. Our church friends have always seen us as very liberal; our "worldly" friends see us as ultraconservative. There's never been any good fit. This past month has taught us to look at this whole thing differently.

I could speak for ages about the family of God worldwide that has rallied around us. Former Bible-study friends we haven't seen in years have written to tell us about Bible-study groups and churches across this nation who lift me up in prayer daily. Missionaries and students around the world who learned of my situation from my brother are praying as well.

Even friends who are nonbelievers have said they're praying for us; they don't know what else to do. They don't know that is the greatest thing they can do! I wonder if God is using my illness to draw these people closer to Himself? I cannot tell you how humbling it is to read and hear these things on a daily basis. E-mails and phone calls are a never-ending encouragement. My feet have not touched the ground since this started—not because I feel so great, but because I feel I'm being carried all the time.

Am I glad I have cancer? Of course not. Would I choose to go back? No. This has allowed our family to experience God's love, through you, in ways we never dreamed possible. And it has allowed so many of you to serve Him in a way that is pleasing to Him. Hebrews 13:16 says, "And do not forget to do good and to share with others, for with such sacrifices God is pleased" (NIV).

God is so pleased with you all! We read in 1 Peter 4:10 that "each one should use whatever gift he has received to serve others, faithfully administering God's grace in its various forms" (NIV). You are literally serving me but pleasing God, bringing meals, babysitting me, driving our son around, e-mailing our daughter in New York to show her you care, sending cards, flowers, gifts, and a team of marvelous women have kept my shop open in spite of knowing nothing about what I do. And I know that you prayed, even if I never heard from you. You lifted me up to God; I could feel it. To you young children who say prayers for Mrs. Richardson, well that's me. I'm the one you're lifting up to God.

Philippians 4:6-7 says, "Do not be anxious about anything, but in everything, by prayer and petition, with thanksgiving, present your requests to God. And the peace of God, which transcends all understanding, will guard your hearts and your minds in Christ Jesus" (NIV). This is what your prayers have truly done for me. You have loved me and served our Lord in the way He has chosen for you right now. And in Jesus' name, I thank you.

We had a similar experience when Ian was diagnosed. We attend a large church and had been feeling lonely in the crowd. Ian's illness changed that. Within days we were in deep with leaders and precious saints we'd never known before. Now hardly a week goes by without us experiencing some sort of intimate conversation with someone from our church.

As an American who sees life through an American cultural grid, I tend to think of faith primarily as something between God and me. It is that, but our family experienced how fragile faith is when it tries to stand alone and how it flourishes when fed by the faith of others.

Some spoke of our faith as if we were towering redwood trees. Not so! We felt like little saplings blown over by the winds of what we saw and heard moment by moment: frightening seizures, medical opinions, test results, and doctors asking questions that pressed us to consider ominous "what ifs."

Here in Colorado we love our aspen groves. What some see as hundreds of solitary aspen trees on a mountainside is actually a colony with a common root system. Individual trees in the grove may live a brief 30 to 150 years. Fire or drought may take down individual trees, but their shared subterranean root systems remain for thousands of years, sprouting fresh life again and again. Renee and I may have felt blown over for a moment, but then our faith was revived by an e-mail, a note, a visit, or a phone call. It was obvious to us that we were not standing alone. Our colony of faith radiates far and wide and deep. And pain—pain shared rather than hidden—was what revealed the roots that were sustaining us.

SILVER LININGS

When we moved to Colorado, I thought the Rocky Mountains would be the most glorious feature of this state. I've been surprised that what most often takes my breath away are the clouds. Nature photographers often come here for the clouds. Have you noticed that clouds are most beautiful as the darkness is approaching or receding? People say that every cloud has a silver lining, an expression derived from John Milton's *Comus,* which says, "Did a sable cloud turn forth her silver lining on the night?"

We see the silver linings only against the backdrop of darkness.

Linda has learned to think about her cancer as a very good thing wrapped up in a very bad thing. She has said that in spite of all that she's suffered, she'd not want to go back to her pre-cancer life. Our family is still in process on that. Our pain is still ripe. But even a few weeks into Ian's illness, I jotted down these silver linings:

- *A big hug from the body.* I used to wonder if people really read my prayer memos. Now I know! The outpouring of love and support and prayer from family and friends has at times been an overwhelming flood. We started pinpointing on a map the nations in which friends were praying for us. The body of Christ around the world has been giving us a big hug.
- *Kindness flowing.* How often I have prayed that my children would just be kind to one another. Now kindness is flowing much more freely. Siblings are actually rising above bickering to truly care for one another. These things are a balm for this father's heart.

- *Experiencing God.* One of the deepest longings of my heart is that my children will experience God. As we've been walking through the valley of tears, God has been stooping down to look each one of us in the eye, meeting each of us in our walk down this difficult path.
- *Lives being transformed.* Just before Ian's illness, we had intensified our prayers for our neighbors. One day, in the intensive care waiting room, one of my colleagues said to one of our neighbors, "Watch this family. They walk with God." And they have watched us closely, eager to help but also curious about what our God is doing with us. Many friends around the world are looking at their own children through new eyes, with fresh recognition of what a gift each child is.

A few weeks later I wrote:

We are marveling at the extraordinary ways that the body of Christ has been pouring out practical support for us. There has been a stream, at times a torrent, of not-so-random acts of kindness.

Ian's siblings have dropped everything to be here in spite of their own responsibilities and the cost of airfare. Aunts and uncles are lining up to do the same for weeks at a time. Our dear friend Lauren is quitting her high-paying job on the East Coast to move in with us just to serve us for a year. How do you say thank you for such things?

My work colleagues have stepped up at great personal sacrifice to free me to focus at home. Local friends have been earnest, generous, and creative in finding ways to lift our load. A friend of our daughter's has practically moved into our home to love on our boys. I don't know how many nights he's slept on our couch.

Friends scattered around the globe pray faithfully, recruit others to pray, and send generous, practical gifts. An Asian senator called my assistant to say, "What does David need?" A Malaysian executive organized an extraordinary gift from his ministry team, even as he himself was facing a frightening health crisis.

Among the greatest silver linings are people who carry us to Jesus every day. I am astounded by their passion and faithfulness. Some tell me that they begin praying before their feet touch the floor in the morning and continue through the day until their last waking moments. I confess that I've rarely prayed for anyone like others have prayed for us. They are gifts from heaven, mobilized by God to carry us.

STRETCHER BEARERS

One intercessor called himself a "stretcher bearer," like the friends who brought the lame man to Jesus in Luke 5. I find real encouragement in that passage.

The story starts, in verse 17, with Luke writing, "The power of the Lord was present . . . to heal" (NIV). We felt that in our experience with Ian. Although our doctors may have felt impotent or frustrated, I sensed the power of the Lord present with us.

Though the crowds surrounding Jesus kept the man's friends from getting to Him the conventional way, they did not give up easily. Faith does not guarantee instant, easy results. Their faith led them to be persistent and creative in seeking God, just as we saw with our stretcher bearers. It seemed like the body of Christ was assailing heaven on our behalf, and often with such creativity — on Facebook sites or in bedside intercession accompanied by a harp or guitar.

Verse 20 says that Jesus saw *their* faith. Throughout Ian's illness, we saw faith on his behalf flooding North America and traversing the globe.

The story in Luke digresses into a theological debate among the religious "experts." Our situation also pressed our theology to the wall. I doubt that the lame man was impressed with the theological precision of the Pharisees. I imagine he was deeply impressed by the love and faith of his friends. Jesus surely was.

In the end, Jesus called on the lame man himself to demonstrate faith. I confess that I don't know how all this works. There is so much mystery here. But somehow I believe that God was watching Ian's response very closely. Did He see faith there? I watched that carefully. Most of the time in those early days Ian was overwhelmed with nausea and pain and weakness. He said that he prayed most when the pain was most severe.

I have to believe that the faith of the lame man's friends spurred him to believe. So when Jesus looked him in the eye and told him to get up, he was caught up in the faith of his friends and in Jesus' obvious authority over his infirmity. Similarly, I watched Ian get caught up in the faith of so many who loved him.

The results? God's glory was displayed. People were astonished. In fact, they were afraid. Something remarkable had happened. Jesus had come to town.

The lame man's friends brought him to Jesus in front of a crowd, and we brought Ian to Jesus right in front of everyone. We chose to live our drama with those around us. God's reputation was on the line. Parents and children and neighbors and churches and friends and doubters and intercessors all over the world were watching. We asked God to show His power and authority once again. And He did.

GANG-TACKLING GOD?

Ian's story became sort of an Internet phenomenon. It ricocheted around the globe from friend to friend, church to church, Bible study to Bible study. We began to see that "six degrees of separation" phenomenon in which someone thousands of miles away would mention Ian's story and find others who already knew and were praying. In the midst of all that, I wrote this in my journal:

What is the significance of having so very many praying for Ian all over the world? I hear of church after church and group after group earnestly praying for him. Hundreds and hundreds of children are praying for him. Even non-Christians are praying for him. This whole thing is stunning to me.

So what is this we're doing? Are we trying to gang-tackle God? Is this like trying to overwhelm the phones at the White House to get the president's attention? If we get enough people praying, will God have to capitulate to us? No, I don't think we're trying to force God's hand. And I'm sure that we already have His full attention.

Rather, I think that we are bringing God great pleasure. There's nothing like the sound of many voices and instruments in harmony. It's beautiful and powerful. We are creating a great symphony of faith and love rising up to His throne. We are merely hearing about this symphony through our prayer map, website, and the hundreds of e-mails I've received. But God actually hears the symphony itself, the blending of children praying simply, parents crying out as if Ian were their own child, strangers loving a child they've never met, and

dear friends pouring out their hearts to God on our behalf.

O Lord, may You find pleasure in this! You are the Concert Master here. You are the Composer and the Conductor. I love You and trust You regardless of how You choose to continue this song.

People praying for Ian all over the world

FAITH TRANSFUSIONS

There's nothing like a rare form of cancer to immerse you in the world of medical realities. Because chemotherapy kills more than cancer, we had to carefully monitor Ian's white blood cells and platelets. If they were too low, we had to isolate him or give him a blood transfusion. We also had to closely monitor his level of pain to manage his narcotics.

While we were watching these indicators, I suspect that God was monitoring something else: our faith. I don't believe that we have some remote control on God, a faith lever that we push to get Him to do what we want. But I know that He pays close attention to our faith. A quick read of the third chapter of Paul's first letter to the Thessalonians shows him checking their faith like a nurse checking a pulse.

And here is where other believers played such a huge role. In our home we were consumed with Ian's care, on top of caring for our other children and the practical things that piled high in the wake of all of Ian's needs. We didn't have a lot of unfilled moments to sit and reflect on faith. Our faith was often expressed on the run. But when we paused with a welcome visitor to pray with Ian, or when we made time to read the letters to Ian from his website or the mail, our faith was stoked.

Some wrote to us saying how my writing was inspiring their faith. Well, that's a two-way street. We were connected at the heart, and our friends were regularly providing us with much-needed faith transfusions.

Like the apostle Paul, we embraced our need for such transfusions: "I long to see you so that I may impart to you some spiritual gift to make you strong—that is, that you and I may be mutually encouraged by each other's faith" (Romans 1:11-12, NIV).

IT'S NOT A GAME ANYMORE

Just as pain ought to draw the body of Christ to one another and to God, so pain should draw families together. Sadly, crisis affects many families like a terrorist bomb rather than a fusing catalyst. Mothers immerse themselves in caring for their child while fathers feel inadequate and alienated. Siblings withdraw, feeling lost among the overwhelming needs or unable to cope with their own hurt and confusion.

I'm thankful that our entire extended family has actually been drawn together through our tragedies. In the week after Ian's death, our house was filled with members from both sides of our family just loving one another. Not since our wedding nearly thirty years ago had this group of people been assembled under one roof, talking, laughing, crying. Linda and I, in particular, have drawn closer together because of our painful journeys. But it wasn't always that way. This is how she explained our relationship to her friends, shortly after we found out about Ian's cancer.

"I'm the boss."

"No, I'm the boss."

"No, I'm the boss because I'm older."

And so it went every time we played, my little brother and me. I was older, so if we played office, I was the boss; he was the secretary. Playing store, I was the manager; he was the clerk. If we played school, I was the teacher; he was the student. Women's rights in the '60s. Yeah!

One day, tired of having a brat for a big sister, David leaned forward with his hands on his hips and yelled, "When we grow up, I'm going to be bigger than you, stronger than you, and older than you!" I laughed at him, saying he might grow stronger and taller, but never older, so he quit. Game over.

Over the years, I watched my "little" brother become a Christian while I remained a wary skeptic. He studied and became a missionary, writer, pastor, and father to seven kids. David was so smart, so rational, and so grown up (so unlike me) that I began to view him as an older brother.

Four days after my cancer was first diagnosed, I had radical surgery at 10 at night. Although David and his wife lived an hour and a half away and had a house full of children, they were right there with Steve that night, waiting and praying. In fact, David took off work for the next three weeks to drive two and a half hours round trip through D.C. traffic to visit me daily.

After his first visit in the ICU, he started to leave, turned back in the doorway, and said, "I love you." Now let me explain that miracle. The Lyons family never said, "I love you." This was a first. It just leaped out of his heart and into his mouth. It was the beginning of a new family tradition. Ah, the good things cancer can do.

The past eight years I've learned more than I ever wanted to know about cancer—the bad and the good—including how it can heal us from lack of faith, self-absorption, and myriad other selfish things. Having cancer can be a severe mercy. I wouldn't wish it on my worst enemy, but neither would I wish away the experience, because that would wish away the blessings.

Dave was my spiritual guide for years, answering nearly every theological question I threw at him. But with cancer, I learned things about God and faith that only come from having a life-threatening disease, things David knew or believed but had never experienced.

Now Ian is living this same battle. My brother now has to face a life I never wanted him to understand, no matter how much it's blessed me. Sometimes I do hold back, not wanting to tell him there's a time to give up trying to control the outcome, just give it to God and He'll care for us. How do you tell a father to "give up" fighting for his son, to trust God to the point of death?

Since Ian's cancer diagnosis, Dave and I are closer than ever. He asks questions; he knows I "get" it. I get the pain, I get the waiting and uncertainty, and I get the reality of living miracles. Until you live it, you can't get it. Recently I wept as I told him, "I never wanted to have this in common with you." He's become my little brother again, calling me his mentor in pain. I wish we could just play office again.

On David's landmark fiftieth birthday, I wrote to him: "David, you were right all along. You're now stronger than me. At six feet, you're much bigger than me. And most certainly, now that you're fifty, you're much older than me!"

In the midst of every crisis, we face choices that lead to either isolation or intimacy. We can hunker down and withdraw, or we can open up and receive. We can pull back and try to cope alone, or we can allow ourselves to be used as a catalyst for grace and love to flow.

Linda wrote about such choices as one of her friends dealt with her own cancer.

October 17, 2007

Marcia,

You will perhaps become tired of hearing this, as I have. However, I look at you and listen to you talk about what is going on in your life, and I see God. I'm not going to "flatter" you by telling you how amazing and strong you are, because we both know it's not you. What I'm seeing is a child who has full confidence in her Father holding her hand as she walks into the fire. A child who is able to take that frightening step in peace.

It's in your eyes and on your face. People who don't know God—your hairdresser, a neighbor, a shop clerk—are going to see that, and God will be glorified in ways you never dreamed. When I was about thirty and still running and screaming away from God, someone gave me a book titled *A Severe Mercy*. It's about a man whose believing wife died, and through that he came to believe in God. A severe mercy to save him. It knocked me over. Being used to glorify God while fighting cancer is somehow a severe mercy. You won't necessarily die, but parts of you will die due to pain, soreness, weariness, inevitable worry, lost hair. In those ways you will die so that others might live. God will be glorified through you. It's an amazing journey, and "I thank my God every time I remember you" (Philippians 1:3, NIV) because He has prepared you to be His servant. You don't have to suffer alone.

You might come to hate it while still being thankful for it, like I have. You said you don't know why He has decided to have you go through this. The reason is here. You are strengthening me, and I've already been through it! Imagine how you'll affect the nonbelievers in your life! Seeing you gives me more courage, because it reminds me how He has been with me. It reminds me to let the small stuff go and concentrate on Him.

Oh, how much we miss if we withdraw into ourselves in response to our pain. How much our family and church may miss. And how much the world misses.

You may be tempted to open up to others but question how they will respond to the challenge. How will you know unless you give them a chance?

One day many years ago, a friend challenged my wife to share with me how deeply disappointed she was with our marriage. Renee was terrified to do it. She was sure I would respond with indignant anger. But her friend explained to Renee that she was not respecting me by assuming I would respond badly. She urged Renee to give me the opportunity to respond well. Renee was so fearful that she melted down as she approached our house. But somehow she overcame her fear and told me the truth. And I did get angry. But only for a short time. Then I came around, and we entered into a season of healing and growth and sweet romance that has continued for decades. What if Renee had refused to give me the opportunity to grow into loving her the way she longed to be loved? We would have missed so much beauty and joy.

When we are in pain, we tend to feel like no one understands. Our need to be loved and Consider coming to *dontwastethepain.com* to connect with others, to share your story, or to join the discussion of others' stories. There you can join a virtual small group led by a mentor. Or you can join as a family, a Sunday school class, or a small group that wants to learn to grow together.

Perhaps God intends to use your tragedy to usher you, and those around you, into beauty and joy that you have never known—yet. Painful junctures in our lives present opportunities for us and for the body of Christ around us: We can be church as it often is, or church as it is designed to be. We can conceal needs, or carry them together. We can allow faith to wither, or share transfusions. We can live in isolation, or we can engage. We can wallow in the ashes, or allow beauty to spring to life once again.

QUESTIONS FOR REFLECTION

- ▶ How is your pain bringing out the best (or the worst) in those around you?
- ▶ How are you doing with letting others love you?
- ▶ Are there questions that you wish people would ask you?

CHAPTER 7

But the Physicians

In the thirty-ninth year of his reign Asa became diseased in his feet. His disease was severe, yet even in his disease he did not seek the LORD, but the physicians. (2 Chronicles 16:12, NASB)

We are deeply aware of the huge debt that we owe to dedicated doctors and nurses who have cared for us and our loved ones, but it was still difficult when early one morning in March 2009, two doctors and two nurses marched into Ian's hospital room, saying, "We'd like to talk about Ian's future—are you ready to discuss removing life support?" Looking down at my son battling for his life, I asked, "Could we have this conversation someplace *else*?"

As a result, three days later Renee and I walked into a formal "care consultation" to discuss Ian's future treatment. Other parents had warned us that this could feel like a court trial where we were fighting for our son's life. We walked into a conference room filled with twelve medical professionals, including four doctors, two nurses, two social workers, a chaplain, and a hospital administrator. Just a little intimidating! Still, we were prepared, and the doctor in charge seemed a little surprised when I read this written statement:

Thank you for the excellent care you have provided for Ian these past thirteen months. We love your people and your facility. You have shown compassion and courage and creativity. You have always given full attention to our needs, even in the midst of responding to so many other intense needs every day. You have gone without sleep and have carried Ian in your heart even when you go home. You have had a major role in keeping Ian alive, and we are deeply grateful.

Now, as we face where to go from here, it is vital that you understand where we are coming from as Ian's parents. It is no secret that we are followers of Jesus. Some may find the ways we express our faith strange or uncomfortable. Others are very comfortable with it. But all of you have always demonstrated the utmost respect. So I feel safe briefly explaining to you a couple of things that are central to how we'll decide our path forward.

First, our faith means we don't desperately cling to Ian's life in this world. Ian has already opened his heart to Jesus and walks with Him. So when Ian goes home to heaven, we know he'll be welcomed into a far better life, although far sooner than we could have expected. It would be a huge and painful loss for us, but we are not desperately or irrationally clinging to Ian's life.

Second, our faith means that we believe God is doing miracles today. You have probably seen some of them yourselves. Ian is already a miracle. No one expected him to live through last spring. Medical statistics said the odds were at least 100-to-1 against his survival then. But he has not only lived, he has thrived. Was that through medical care? Nutritional therapy? Was it something God did apart from natural means? A surgeon we know in Oklahoma often says all healing is a gift from God. Sometimes God works through medicine and medical professionals. Sometimes He works more directly, through what we call "supernatural means." But all healing is a gift from God. In Ian's case, we believe God is working through both natural and supernatural means.

We proceeded with a vigorous discussion about Ian's care—and even some laughter when I asked if Ian could "flunk out" of hospice care through a miraculous recovery. Altogether, it was an appropriate, though exhausting, encounter.

Ian's nurses

I hope that you never have to face such a meeting. But it is likely that at some point in your life, you will need to think through the implications of your faith as it applies to the medical profession. You will wrestle with who and what to trust with your life or the life of one you love. You will want to be rescued by doctors, medicines, alternative treatments, or those gifted in supernatural healing. You will search for wisdom for the hardest decisions you may ever face. You will grope for some way to control your situation. Pain, perhaps more than anything else, makes us desperate for control.

MY PART AND GOD'S PART

After nine years of chemotherapy and three surgeries, Linda has learned some important lessons in sorting out her part, God's part, and the role of medical professionals:

"Take two aspirin and call me in the morning." It's such a trivial response to our pain that it's become a joke. We want more than

temporary relief; we want to be healed, and we want someone to make us better. Now.

If we eat right, exercise, avoid stress, sugar, and overindulgence, follow doctors' orders, take our meds, undergo all the tests, and have all the surgeries, will we be healed? Is doing the "right thing" ever guaranteed to heal us? It helps, but, no. I know people who've gone the all-natural route in health care, and they're healed (unless they're not). I know people who undergo all the accepted medical procedures, take all the prescribed meds, and they're healed (or they're not). That might seem random, but God is not random. He is in control of our medical realities, and He is the one who heals. Because He has given us power and authority through the Holy Spirit, He also gives us a role in our healing. It's a role—through obedience and prayer—but it's not control. Peace comes when we finally get real and accept that.

I can certainly do things to make myself feel better for the moment. I can and should follow my doctor's advice, take my meds, and eat the right kinds of food. I also understand those who feel they have to do everything in their power to battle their disease. But if I believed that I was personally in control of my own healing, then anxiety and bitterness would grow as I continued to fail at that. My life would be frustrating and wasted as I found I was unable to cure myself by my own actions. I'd feel like a passenger on an airplane who suddenly realized that the pilot had died and I had to land the plane myself. Yikes! I don't know how to do this! I'm not trained! I have no idea what to do with these controls! If I mess up, I'm going to die! "Hello? Hello? Can somebody help me!" Fortunately, God is in charge of healing. And when He heals, He tells me how to play my part. It's so much easier—and better—to lean into what God Himself wants to do with my sickness.

It's easier to live with cancer and other sources of pain when we know that we are in God's hands. The final outcome is not up to us, or our doctors, or even the effectiveness of medicine. It's up to Him.

I love what we see in our friends in Costa Rica. When they get sick, their first response is to pray! Sadly, for most Americans (Christians and non-Christians alike), our first response is to go to the medicine cabinet or the drug store or the health food store or—if it's really serious—to call the doctor. Our Costa Rican friends use doctors, too. But we can learn a lot from their first response.

God is in control of healing, but we do have responsibilities. Our first responsibility is to pray. Part of our prayer for Ian was that he would grow into the faith and maturity to play his part in praying for his own healing, along with the thousands who were praying with him. The next part was for him to take personal responsibility for the restoration of his health, which is not always at the forefront of a teenage boy's mind. While we embraced chemo as God's means and our responsibility, it did a lot of damage while it was working so hard to kill the cancer cells. An oncologist in Texas, Dr. Jairo Oliveras, taught us nutritional therapy to rebuild Ian's strength during chemotherapy. We went after that aggressively, and God blessed our work. Over the next year, again and again Ian "beat the odds" and left his primary oncologist marveling at how well he handled chemotherapy and was able to live a relatively normal life.

It was not easy for Ian to give up things he loved to eat and to wolf down more than one hundred nutritional-supplement capsules a day. It required a huge amount of self-discipline rarely found in a twelve-year-old. In time he regarded it as routine and shrugged it off as a small thing. Worry? No, that wasn't part of Ian's psyche. Take responsibility for his part? Ian did that well.

BLESSINGS VERSUS MIRACLES

There is a popular faith healer in our town. He has a television and radio ministry and travels the world doing crusades. I generally don't pay much attention to such people, but we have a dear friend who works for this man. In the midst of Ian's illness, she brought me a recording of one of his messages, a message I did not expect from such a person.

He distinguished miracles from blessings. I don't fully agree with his use of the words, but I do agree with the point he was trying to make: As he explained it, a "miracle" is God's supernatural intervention, but a "blessing" is God's favor flowing toward those who follow His instructions. The speaker chided those who ignore God's instructions, then expect Him to rescue them with a miracle. Some people do this with their finances. They don't follow God's instructions to discipline their spending and saving, then they expect God to rescue them when they miss a paycheck or have an unexpected expense. Others do this with their health. They don't discipline themselves to care for the body God has entrusted to them, then they expect Him to rescue them when it begins to break down.

Thankfully, God is merciful. He is often generous with miracles, even when we have not disciplined ourselves to follow His instructions. But He also expects us to learn from our mistakes. When people receive financial help from our church, they are required to take a course to teach them principles of financial management. And when I go to the doctor for high blood pressure, he gives me instructions regarding diet and exercise. In both cases, those instructions are a gift from God, who is trying to lead us into His blessing. He's giving us responsibility for our part. It's not that God only helps those who help themselves, but He does say that we reap what we sow (see Galatians 6:7).

Still, there's another theme in God's story. It surfaces again and again when God leads us beyond our own ability and teaches us to rely on *His* ability. Our destiny will always exceed our own ability. Our opportunities will also exceed our own ability, and God often prepares us for such opportunities through difficult circumstances. When those come in the form of a health crisis, we have choices to make regarding where we will place our faith.

THE PLACE OF THOSE WHO "PRACTICE" MEDICINE

In the past decade, Linda has spent more time immersed in the medical community than just about anyone I know. While admiring and appreciating her doctors, she's never questioned who is responsible for her healing.

What about those who skip the doctor altogether? We've all heard stories of people who do that, even parents who risk being held liable for abuse or neglect when they don't seek medical treatment for their sick children. Why not just ignore the doctor and go straight to God for healing? Isn't it up to Him anyway?

Some doctors are certainly tools used by God to serve His own purpose, to minister to those who are in need, and it is no insult to God to go to them for help. Some may take credit for healing; others know they are at the mercy of what God allows. A good friend who is a neurologist, referring to those who put so much faith in a good doctor, told us, "People would be horrified if they knew how little we really know." And this man is brilliant, tops in his field. He knows a lot, but he knows his own limitations. And he knows no one can ever know it all. That he is willing to acknowledge this makes me trust him more.

There's only so much we can do to bring about our own healing naturally. We are limited beings. Remember when Jesus said, "With man this is impossible, but with God all things are possible" (Matthew 19:26, NIV)? I take comfort in knowing the power to be healed—or even to feel better—need not lie within my own abilities or even my doc's. As George Carlin once quipped, how long does a physician have to "practice" before she or he gets it right, anyway?

SONGS OR SWORDS

A month after Ian's initial diagnosis, I was reflecting on the interaction between supernatural healing and physical science.

From David's Journal
March 4, 2008

> Yesterday was disappointing. Today is better. Yesterday nausea from the chemotherapy overwhelmed Ian. And we were thinking, *Is this the way it's going to be for the next three weeks?* Today we're using other medications to deal with the side effects, and Ian has improved. He's able to sit up, and he actually ate a popsicle.
>
> So what does this year ahead hold for us? It's been thrilling to see such dramatic healing so far. But even when we see a 99 percent reduction in the tumor, we'll need to press on until the cancer is 100 percent gone. Will God do that quickly? I don't know. I pray that He will. But I am also preparing my heart for a longer road.
>
> I think of how God defeated Jehoshaphat's enemies with songs of praise, but He defeated David's enemies with conventional swords. God chooses His means and His timing. In a culture infatuated with immediate results, we beg God for shortcuts, while knowing He may have a longer battle in store for us. We also know that God has a flair for the mercifully swift climax.
>
> Tonight I pray toward two horizons. I pray that God will relieve the nausea so that Ian can eat and rebuild his strength. But I also pray that God will completely remove the causes of that nausea in such a way that all will know there must be a God in heaven.

Here's the thing. God is the healer, the Great Physician. He says, "I, the LORD, am your healer" (Exodus 15:26, NASB). He is Jehovah Rapha, "*the Lord who heals.*" Jesus healed all who came to Him for healing. That was perhaps the main reason so many came out to see Him. It's one of the main things that made Him famous in Galilee and Judea. And He said, "If you've seen Me, you've seen the Father" (see John 14:9). Healing is a big deal to God. It's not a sideshow or a freak show, like some television evangelist shows.

Sometimes God does heal directly and supernaturally. But often He heals indirectly through doctors, nurses, medicines, nutrition, and alternative treatments. The Healer has many means.

DISEASE REVEALS THE HEART

I'm looking out the window of my study, and I see Pikes Peak covered with snow. When we moved into this house, a dear friend looked out this same window and gave me this passage: "I lift up my eyes to the hills—where does my help come from? My help comes from the LORD, the Maker of heaven and earth" (Psalm 121:1-2, NIV).

In the midst of Ian's illness, I personalized this passage this way: "We lift our eyes to the physicians, nurses, chemotherapy, and nutritional therapy—but where does our help come from? Our help comes from the LORD, the Maker of heaven and earth." In other words, we love our physicians and nurses, and we'll do our best with chemotherapy and nutritional therapy. But Ian's Maker is the One who will heal him.

King Asa, from the book of 2 Chronicles, drifted to another perspective. Early in life, Asa had been a great man of faith. When facing an Ethiopian army of a million, outnumbered more than 2-to-1, he prayed:

> LORD, there is no one besides You to help in the battle between the powerful and those who have no strength; so help us, O LORD our God, for we trust in You, and in Your name have come against this multitude. O LORD, You are our God; let not man prevail against You. (14:11, NASB)

But later in life something had shifted in Asa's heart: "His disease was severe, yet even in his disease he did not seek the LORD, but the physicians" (16:12, NASB).

Asa's example is sobering. He's not so different from most of us. It's so easy to drift into depending on something or someone other than God. Mindful of this, whenever we administered medicine or therapy to Ian, we also laid hands on him and prayed. This reminded us of who the Healer really is.

PRAYING FOR YOUR DOCTOR

What if Asa had sought the Lord *and prayed* for his physicians?

It is hard for me to imagine the weight of responsibility a surgeon bears when he cuts open someone's body. Whether or not they know it, surgeons need God's help. Praying for our doctors is one of the most practical ways we can work out this dilemma of entrusting so much to them while depending entirely on God. This journal entry of Linda's, written a few days after her third surgery, illustrates this:

February 2, 2002

It's interesting that with this surgery I asked people to specifically pray for Dr. Boice and not me. It seemed odd that I couldn't think of anything for people to pray for me. The reason why revealed itself the evening of the surgery.

Surgery was scheduled for around 7 p.m., and we had to arrive a few hours early for prep. While I was lying on the gurney waiting to be wheeled into the operating room, someone came in to tell me it would be awhile. Dr. Boice was still assisting with another surgery that had begun at 10 that morning, and things weren't going well. What? My oncologist was going to perform surgery on me after already being in a difficult surgery all day? Great.

Dr. Boice didn't finish until after 10 and finally met me in the OR around 11 p.m. He had to have been exhausted. Yet my surgery went smoothly, and the results were excellent. The highlight for me came the following morning. Around 7 a.m., although I was not ready to be awake, Dr. Boice came bounding in. I don't know if I've ever seen him so energized and happy. I asked if he was exhausted after such a long previous day, and he said he felt "great" and was thrilled with the ease and the results of my surgery. This, after nearly fourteen straight hours of surgery and very little sleep.

I thought back to all the people who had promised to pray for this doctor and silently thanked God for guiding me to ask for that prayer. It was comforting to picture God guiding his hands and strengthening him all along.

We can pray that God will strengthen and enable our doctors. We can also pray that He will change their minds. "The king's heart is like channels of water in the hand of the LORD; He turns it wherever He wishes" (Proverbs 21:1, NASB).

If that's true for kings, it's true for doctors, too. While I don't believe that God flips some remote-control switch to change a doctor's thinking, I do believe He will prod them in another direction when it serves His purposes. Of course, Satan can prod a doctor's thinking, too, and we have to stand against that.

In March 2008, Ian's oncologist had given us a twelve-month road map for treatment, which called for radiation and surgery in July

Ian's oncologist

and August. But by June we were already seeing miraculous progress. Wanting a specific prayer target, I asked the oncologist what kind of progress he would have to see to change his mind about the radiation and surgery. After a long pause he said, "In Ian's case I cannot imagine a scenario in which I would not recommend those procedures." I was disappointed. We really did not want to take Ian through radiation and surgery. Yet we couldn't see ourselves refusing those treatments when the doctor felt they were needed. So the doctor became the beneficiary of our prayers. With such an aggressive and dangerous cancer, it was very unlikely that the doctor would risk forgoing these treatments. Merely healing Ian would not be enough; we were asking God to heal Ian *and* change the doctor's mind.

I'll never forget receiving the call from our oncologist: "There is no sign of the tumor, and the bone marrow tests show 0.00 percent cancer." Feeling bold, I asked about the radiation and surgery. Without hesitating he said, "I don't think those will be necessary." God had not only healed Ian, He had led the doctor to change his mind in spite of the professional risks that implied. Now that's a miracle!

"TRUSTING" YOUR DOCTOR

In one of her more vulnerable moments, Linda had to ask herself if she merely trusted her doctor, or if she was putting all her faith in him.

I was ill, physically and mentally exhausted. Two of our vehicles needed professional help; there were many unsolved problems with the closing of my former business that needed attention; I was dealing with multiple weekly hospital visits, unexplained headaches, and was at my wit's end. On the way home from yet another physical therapy session, the car I was driving said, "I quit."

I called Larry, our knight in shining armor (make that shining tow truck), yet one more time. As I waited for him, my cell phone rang. It was my oncologist's office, telling me that my doctor, who had cared for me for the past eight years, was moving his practice out of Annapolis.

I went from faithful servant to insane, screaming woman.

I was NOT going to let this happen! Over my dead body (okay, bad phrase) would I lose him. I trusted and needed him; no one else could care for me as he has. He knows me; I know him. With three to four other hospital visits per week and my life at stake, I absolutely could not deal with this. "He can't leave me," I sobbed.

Then the fit ended as quickly as it had started. God heard me cry out to Him, and I went from desperate panic to complete peace when He uttered these words into my head: "Be still, and know that I am God" (Psalm 46:10, NIV). I sat still. I remembered Romans 8:28: "In all things God works for the good of those who love him, who have been called according to his purpose" (NIV). Before Larry even arrived, I gave it all up. No, I was not going to "let this happen." It was going to happen because God is still in control of my life. I trusted Dr. Boice, but I trusted God more. If I had to find another oncologist, God would guide me to that person. I know who controls my life, and as much "faith" as I have in Dr. Boice, I know it's not him.

GOD'S SECOND OPINION

For years our father battled back pain and high blood pressure. Like the woman who suffered with a hemorrhage for twelve years, he *"endured much at the hands of many physicians"* (Mark 5:26, NASB). Yet he would get upset if we would ever question anything that a doctor told him. Others are on the opposite end of this spectrum, demonizing doctors. I'd rather begin with the assumption that a doctor may be God's instrument to help me. But he is not God, even if he thinks he is.

We tend to look at a doctor's prognosis as a pronouncement from on high. Yet no matter how much confidence doctors may have in their treatment and training, we still call the advice they give a medical "opinion." Ian's oncologists, who are believers, were very aware of the "but God" factor. God Himself had a second "opinion" about Ian's prognosis. And His opinion is always true, an accurate reflection of reality.

It's easier to trust doctors who recognize that their opinions are just opinions, as Linda discovered when God weighed in on her treatment with an opinion of His own:

> I recently changed chemo drugs. The previous drug was lab tested as the most effective in fighting my particular cancer. But once we used it, it was a complete and unexpected failure. The results were clear: Not only did it not work, it allowed the cancer to grow exponentially. Fortunately, Dr. Boice is not the type to insist he knows it all when my body seems to have a mind of its own. He knows it's no reflection on him when God has other ideas. The smartest medical people are the ones who know they don't know it all. They're the ones I trust. I take joy in the times God goes against what is "expected" and surprises us.

A "LEANING OVER" GOD

Our experience with Ian taught us how intimidating a hospital atmosphere can be. There is a military-like discipline that is necessary among medical professionals. Doctors expect to be obeyed by nurses and aides; when they're not, lives are at risk. But that expectation can spill over onto their patients and come across as arrogance.

I am impressed with Dr. Ben Carson, a prominent neurosurgeon. In his book *Think Big*, he talked about how some surgeons can become prima donnas, strutting around expecting others to bow to their authority, and how such behavior is often rooted in insecurity about their abilities or self-worth. He also pointed out how arrogant people tend to stop learning and thus lose competency.

By way of contrast, he described one operating-room experience when four-year-old Christine inexplicably went into cardiac arrest:

As my hands moved quickly, I was silently praying, *Lord, I don't know what's going on or what caused this. Fix it, God, please!*

Then my hands firmly gripped Christine's frail body. I had to turn her over to pump her chest (which couldn't be done from the back without injuring her spine). I paused momentarily before I flipped her over. In that instant, her heart started back up again.

"Thank you, Lord," I said aloud. "I don't know what happened, but clearly You fixed it." We were able to proceed without any further difficulty.

We never did figure out what had happened; perhaps it does not matter. What does matter is: I am convinced that God heard my prayer and intervened for young Christine. This is not to say that I count on pulling off a miracle every time something goes wrong. I follow the simple principle that God cares about every area of our lives, and God wants us to ask for help.[1]

Dr. Carson often speaks of sensing God guiding his hands, like a father leaning over the shoulders of his child. That's what I want my doctors to experience.

My friend Russ shared with me an extraordinary experience he had as a teen. A skiing accident had caused his hip to come apart to the point that he would not be able to walk again without risky surgery. The surgery would require his doctor to twist his leg, forcing it into place. If he twisted too gently, it would not work. If he twisted too hard, it would damage tissues beyond repair. The doctor told him that the best he could hope for was 60 percent success. And he wouldn't know whether it was successful until months after the surgery.

At that point in his life, Russ was painfully shy. So he was alarmed when God prompted him to say something bold to the surgeon before the surgery. He hoped the anesthesia would knock him out before the surgeon showed up. But God kept him awake long enough to overcome his fear and say to the surgeon, "God will be with you, helping you."

A few months after the surgery Russ went in for his follow-up appointment. The doctor told him that the surgery was 100 percent successful, not just 60 percent. He was surprised when the surgeon, who was from India, then pulled out a large photo of his guru and started talking about him. Russ was doubly surprised when the surgeon said, "When I was doing your surgery, I had a powerful sense that God's hands were guiding my hands. Please tell me about your God who was guiding my hands." He did not know those hands, but he sensed their presence. Then he sat there patiently while a shy teenager told him about Jesus Christ, the Great Physician.

As we spent many weeks in intensive care with Ian, we saw how much of medicine is educated guessing, experimenting, and giving things a good try. We also came to deeply appreciate the years of training and experience that enabled our doctors and nurses to guess well. But above all, we saw God leaning over their shoulders.

"MIRACLE CURE" OR GOD'S TIMING?

An old friend of Linda's sent her a copy of the *National Enquirer* and told her to read one story, saying that it was actually true. *Yeah, sure,* she thought as she read the headline: "Mom walks for first time in 31 years—just four hours after taking one little pill!" A woman who had been wheelchair bound most of her life went to a neurologist, who gave her a pill. Later that day she climbed out of her wheelchair and walked for the first time in years. A real-life miracle? Well, yes and no.

The neurologist in the story was Linda's friend, Tony, the one who sent her the article. The story was indeed true. With an unquenchable thirst for knowledge, Tony, a neurologist, likes to attend seemingly obscure lectures on medical research, always hoping to learn something new. He'd attended a conference the week before this woman "happened" to come into his office. She had the exact symptoms he had learned about, and her rare disease was fresh in his mind. He quickly diagnosed her and was able to accurately prescribe the right medicine for her. She walked later the same day for the first time in years. He also diagnosed her daughter with the same inherited disorder and saved her from a lifetime in a wheelchair. Needless to say, the woman and her family were stunned and thrilled. They thought Tony was a miracle worker.

Miracle? To the woman it was. To the *National Enquirer* it was a great story. To Tony, it was the thrill of a lifetime to make such a difference. But who or what cured her — the pills or Tony? Or, was it God? Tony will tell you it wasn't him, but the timing. He was thrilled to be a part of that experience, but he would never say he "cured" her. He was in the right place at the right time, and so was the woman. God is the one who put it all together, but He allowed Tony to get the credit. Coincidence is that for which God does not bother to take credit.

HEALERS

God can heal through many means. But we must not confuse the means with the Healer.

Desperate people sometimes turn to desperate means. We're all familiar with charlatans who claim to be able to heal whatever ails you. There will always be peddlers of "snake oil" and such things. And there will be those who claim powers from God that they do not possess. But that does *not* mean that God does *not* give the gift of miraculous healing. I believe that He does, even today. I realize this is hard for some to accept or believe. If that's you, please hang in there with me for a moment because I'm going to land on something that is vital and on which I think we can agree.

God sometimes breaks through the time/space continuum and does a healing miracle. In fact, He does this a lot more than many of us know. I used to think this happened only on the frontiers of the gospel.

Anyone familiar with how the gospel is moving among Muslims knows there is a prevailing pattern of Muslims coming to Jesus through visions and dreams. And other Muslims are coming to Jesus through miraculous healing, much like we read about in the Gospels. Just a few weeks ago my daughter witnessed this in Mozambique. With her own eyes she saw a Muslim tribal chief healed from a deformity caused by a machete accident. The next day he brought his entire village to see the *Jesus* film.

But I've witnessed God's miraculous healing in even my own context. While we were in the hospital, a family from our church was waiting for their son to die in an adjacent ward. He was clinically brain dead after a suicide attempt. But a friend, who happens to have a PhD in psychology, came to pray for this young man, and God healed him. The next day he walked out of the hospital.

On a more personal (if less spectacular) level, an acquaintance from California came to pray for Ian. He told us he'd seen many people healed in response to his prayers but was also careful to tell us that not everyone he prayed for was healed. After he'd finished praying for Ian without any apparent effect, he asked if anyone else needed healing. I guess that Renee was in a "Why not?" mood and told him about a shoulder injury that for years had kept her from being able to raise her arm above her head. After she demonstrated the problem, this friend prayed. Immediately Renee's pain disappeared, and the mobility of her arm was restored and remains restored to this day. This stirred some excitement, and as he left, he said that he thought God had done that just to encourage us to believe that, in His time, He would heal Ian also.

Now, if you are like me, you are mentally calculating possible natural explanations for these things. That's okay. Here's my point: Whether you are a Muslim tribal chief or a boy with cancer or a mother with a lame shoulder, God's desire is that you put your faith in Him rather than in any healer. I believe that God sometimes—even often—does bring healing through the prayers of His people. I even believe that

He'd like to do more of that if we'll ask more. But if anyone starts putting his or her faith in the one praying rather than in God Himself, God is not pleased.

THE KING HAS ONE MORE MOVE

In late February 2009, Ian's cancer had crossed the blood-brain barrier and was attacking his brain in earnest. Ian was pressing on with life in spite of the progression of disabilities that were taking over. He hiked up mountains (with a limp), played with his friends, laughed and made us laugh. Then suddenly he fell into seizures one night in the middle of a play rehearsal with a thousand cast members standing nearby. He was rushed to the hospital and may not have lived through the night without serious intervention. That launched us into our most difficult interactions with medical professionals, including the "care consultation" I described earlier. A month later it was becoming clear that this time the cancer was not being defeated by chemotherapy, and we were running out of medical options. I wrote to our praying friends:

March 25, 2009

> *"There's really nothing more that I can do."* These are not words you want to hear from your oncologist. But it has finally come down to that. The MRI yesterday indicated that in spite of the intravenous and intrathecal (spinal fluid) chemotherapy, Ian's brain looks worse. All of us are taking this as a clear indication that this time God is not using chemotherapy to heal Ian.
>
> Is that checkmate? Is this where we give up hope?
>
> We're in what chess players call the endgame. I used to be a serious chess player. Our team won the state championship, and at nationals I even met Bobby Fischer. My favorite opening is called the Queen's Gambit. In that opening, you take a risk right up front, on

your second move. You move your queen bishop pawn out without protecting it. It looks so vulnerable. Experienced opponents know that grabbing that pawn would be a big mistake, but it's a risk nonetheless.

I feel like God did that with us. He opened this game, put us in a high-risk position, then told us to play it out. (He could have led Israel directly out of Egypt, but instead He led them on a circuitous route that left them pinned down by the Red Sea. Why? So He could show them His glory by delivering them from the impossible situation into which He had deliberately led them!) For years He has led our family to live our lives out in the open, transparently sharing our joys and sorrows, our victories and defeats, with those who pray for us. Then He led us down the cancer road with Ian and surrounded us with a growing army of prayer warriors around the world.

I want to make something very clear. We are not driven by fear of Ian's death. It would be a very traumatic loss, but that is not our focus. All along we've said that we will not take desperate measures to avoid the possibility of Ian's death. Neither are we driven by fear of caring for Ian long term in his current condition. The cost would be huge in every way. It staggers us. But we're resolved to follow wherever God leads. Our posture continues to be, "Not our will but Yours." If it were God's will to take Ian home, that would not destroy us or our faith. We'd struggle, but we'd still love and trust Him. We know Him too well. Yet we are convinced that God will heal Ian. He just has not given us the details of how and when.

A few days ago our daughter-in-law posted one sentence in our online guest book—a sentence that rang out like a cannon shot across the bow of the Enemy: "The king ALWAYS has one more move." In a chess game that is not true. By definition, checkmate means that the king is threatened and cannot move out of check. The king has no more moves. But Christi was not talking about chess. She was talking about life! And she was talking about the King of the universe. When Jesus was crucified, Satan thought he had won the game. But the King always has one more move.

So here we are. Medicine has run out of moves. And we're waiting for the King.

And God did move. In spite of ongoing seizures, we soon took Ian home to care for him. Once again, the doctors were amazed. Without chemotherapy, for no apparent medical reason, the cancer began to recede. It was a fierce battle, but against all odds Ian at times actually began to walk and talk. Then one morning the neurologist called to tell us that Ian's EEG showed no seizures. Not only that, but his brain waves, though still very slow, were becoming more organized; when he was asleep, they were almost normal.

The neurologist called this surprising. I called it miraculous. He said that although he's not an oncologist, this would indicate to him that the brain tumors were under control. *Under control of what—or whom?* Ian had not had chemotherapy or anything to treat the cancer in weeks and weeks. Ten weeks earlier doctors had given him three to six weeks to live. Three weeks earlier when we came home from the hospital we were told that without treatment the cancer would probably take him down in days to weeks.

We were beyond anything medicine would do, and it looked like God Himself was stepping in. We were excited.

But the very day after the encouraging neurologist report, an ambulance rushed Ian to the hospital again. The cancer had surfaced in his lungs and was beginning to suffocate him. Although we were back in intensive care, we were far from ready to give up. As I stayed by Ian's bed praying through that weekend for what only God could do, far away in Texas, our friend Kathy Gray was writing this song just for Ian:

> The doctors are grim and their news weighs heavy,
> The room starts to spin and his gait is unsteady,
> He looks at his boy in the bed as he says he
> Doesn't know how much more they can take

He senses the warmth of her hand on his shoulder,
He looks at his bride and begins to feel bolder,
She reminds him what the Father has told her,
And the hope resonates . . .
The King still has one more move!
And I told you His Love would see this through,
Keep believing in spite of your unbelief
And My Spirit will comfort and bring you relief
And faith will reveal what you cannot see
That the King still has one more move!

The next morning, Ian was welcomed into heaven by a great cloud of witnesses. That was not the move we expected.

God says yes to our prayers, but He also says no. We'll look more closely at that in the next two chapters. No matter what the outcome, our family saw that, when tested, our hope was not in medical professionals, medicines, therapies, or even those gifted in supernatural healing. They all have a role to play, but ultimately our hope is not in this life. Our hope transcends this life and eventually lands us in heaven for eternity. The King always has one more move, and our hope must be in Him alone.

QUESTIONS FOR REFLECTION

- ▶ What is your first response when you or someone you love gets sick? How would you like to respond?
- ▶ What do you think may be your doctor's attitude toward God?
- ▶ How is God leading you to pray specifically for your doctor?

CHAPTER 8

PRAYING IN
THE FACE OF PAIN

L *ord, teach us to pray.*
This is a dangerous request. It's dangerous because one of the best ways to learn to pray is to become desperate. And pain is the express train to get there. It's not a pleasant place when you arrive, but you may find—as Linda and I have—that the prayer lessons there make the trip somehow worth it.

Over the past nine years, Linda and those who love her have taken God's graduate course in prayer. We've experienced firsthand what it means to pray with desperation, to pray for the impossible, and to see God break through in the most amazing ways.

From Linda's Journal
November 2000, 6 weeks after initial surgery

When I left the hospital, my CA-125 was down to 1,100—still a bad number but only a fraction of what it had been before surgery. After one round of chemo, it dropped to 900. Today, after a second infusion, I learned the newer results. I'd been praying for a miracle, something near 450, an improbable and preposterous drop of 50 percent. I knew it was unlikely, but it didn't matter. I prayed for the impossible. It's easy to do when you know you'll die without it. And with God, nothing is impossible, right?

While praying, I remained realistic enough to ask God to prepare me for whatever He had planned. Every point on a CA-125 matters, and to be honest, I'd have been content with a measly five-point drop. Prepared to keep my disappointment in check, I was ready to receive any outcome. After all, I was stage IIIC, and this was only the second round of chemo. I had to be realistic.

I sat with my oncologist, who pulled out my test results and looked them over. Suddenly he leaned his head forward, a look of what I read as concern on his face. He didn't speak for a moment. Then he asked, "Has anyone gone over this with you yet?" Clearly, I was dead. "No," I muttered, hanging my head. "What does it say?"

"48. Your CA-125 is only 48." The proverbial pin could have dropped and shattered my eardrums.

WHAT? How could that be? I was at death's door, and now I was almost cancer free? Impossible. My heart was in my throat. Why was God blessing me? Dare I believe He was healing me?

WHAT DID YOU EXPECT?

The coming months unfolded into five years of remission. Linda allowed herself to believe that the cancer was gone forever. She was wrong. By January 2005, her CA-125 began to rise slightly—just enough to plant that speck of concern in the back of her mind, where it lingered for six months. Ready to fight it, she wrote this in July to her friends:

> It's time to pray again. I'm facing four options: (1) Laparo-scopic surgery to remove tumor; (2) Laproscopic surgery leading to normal surgery with tumor removal and chemo; (3) Normal surgery revealing an inoperable web of tumors, which means close me up and send me home; (4) Then

there's always Door Number Four: Just be healed. I'd like door four, please.

Soon after, our niece suggested a corporate prayer meeting of family and close friends to ask God for complete healing. This is how Linda shared the idea with all of us:

Linda in remission

I feel a bit weird even asking you to join us for this corporate prayer thing. After all, I'm asking God to do a miracle. Does He still do those? We can't literally get together in one place (Colorado, Maryland, London, Russia), so let's do it in our own homes at 9 p.m. Tuesday, three days before surgery. In the meantime, I have to get my mind in the right place, to become someone who has the "faith to be healed." Remember when Paul wrote of the man who had that kind of faith (Acts 14:9)? How on earth do I get that?

I think a lot about healing: Do I dare go out on this limb, to actually ask God to suddenly heal me? I don't want surgery. I don't want chemo. I want to be healed. If I believe in healing, then I should be healed, right? If I don't ask for it, it won't happen. What do I have to lose? Can I be that brazen? Will that limb I'm trusting actually hold me as I go out on it? This is scary. I should tell people I believe I'll be healed. If I don't speak it out loud, it won't be true. If I tell Steve, he'll think I'm crazy. I have to just do it. Believe it. Believe God can and will do it.

Is any one of you sick? He should call the elders of the church to pray over him and anoint him with oil in the name of the Lord. And the prayer offered in faith will make the sick person well; the Lord will raise him up. If he has sinned, he will be forgiven. Therefore confess your

145

> sins to each other and pray for each other so that you
> may be healed. The prayer of a righteous man is powerful
> and effective. (James 5:14-16, NIV)

> If I really believe these words are true, then I have to go ahead
> with this. What other choice do I have? Interestingly, the more I
> state out loud that I am healed, the more I believe it. I've gone
> from hoping to believing.

Linda was looking for others to believe with her. She shared this with
her congregation:

> I read a story once about a small midwestern town suffering
> through a long drought. They needed rain soon. The local preacher
> called his flock together one night so they could pray for rain and
> save the suffering farmers. Everyone agreed that it was time to act.
> Sitting around waiting was no longer an option.
> As they gathered in the church, everyone was excited to finally
> do something, to pray for rain. The preacher watched them hurry
> in, happy and animated. A little girl sat down in the front row, and
> he paused to look at her, moved by what he saw. As he quieted the
> crowd, he thought of the faith of this child. While all the adults had
> come hoping their prayers "might" make it rain, the little girl had
> come carrying her umbrella, knowing it would.
> Please pray for me with your umbrellas open.

Our corporate prayer for Linda happened three days before her surgery.
Though she experienced nothing out of the ordinary herself that night,
others did.

> I know a lot of people prayed last night. They prayed believing it
> would matter. Some said they experienced a strong wind as they
> prayed. Could that have been the Holy Spirit anointing their prayers?

I woke up full of confidence today, believing I'll go into that hospital on Friday, and there will be no tumor. I mentioned it to Steve, who said, "Uh-huh," perhaps afraid to hope for too much. But I'm not hoping; I know. After the anointing and all that prayer, what else could I expect?

People were anxious to hear of the miraculous results from my blood test today, but there were none. The cancer appears to be getting worse. Everyone was disappointed but not necessarily surprised. I'd asked for a miracle, but it hadn't come. All I could think was, *Hey, did anyone ask God to heal me in twelve hours? No? I didn't think so. Blood test be darned, I'm healed.* The blood test just didn't show it yet. The only bad thing is that I'll still have to have surgery to prove there's no tumor.

Two days later, Linda was lying on a gurney outside the operating room.

Before surgery, I was smiling like a goofball and nearly giddy with excitement. Should I tell someone it's already gone, that they don't need to do this? Will they think I'm a nut? AM I a nut?

The surgery started at 9:30 p.m. By 11:30, Dr. Boice was making his way to Steve in the waiting room to tell him what he'd found: Nothing! Nada! Zip! Dr. Boice was amazed. He had expected to find my body filled with disease, yet he found absolutely no sign of any cancer. He had no explanation for the incremental increases in my CA-125 count or the hot spot on the PET scan, but he said that I could go home as soon as I was up to it, and at this point we would do nothing more. Nothing! No chemo! Praise God.

After the surgery and news of the miracle, my wife, Renee, shared a story that she had been keeping to herself until after Linda's surgery. During our time of corporate prayer, Renee had felt a strong wind blow up around her. Terrified and shaking, she knew she was in the presence of the Lord, and He was telling her that it would be as Linda asked. Renee was not alone in experiencing God in a tangible way that night we prayed. You see, our prayers aren't just about healing for the sick. They're also used to bring the people praying into a more personal experience with God. Linda was later able to explain that to her church congregation.

A river runs along the bank as it courses down its path. Most of us will remember the river, but not so its banks. There might be places we notice, but it's the river that matters, the river that carries the power of the water, the river that runs to the sea, the river that transports people and goods. It's the river that has the name. It's the river we remember.

I don't want to be the river. (I'm not the river.) I want to be the bank along the river of God. I hope He's using me to reveal Himself to the world, to show His glory and power, but I myself am incidental. I know I'll change as He touches me, but that's between Him and me. In real life, when engineers try to change or control the course of a river by shoring up its banks or making architectural changes, it's the river that ultimately determines its own course. The river has all the power. God has all the power. He uses us; we can't control or change Him.

What He's done in my life is amazing. Then again, it's not. It's what He does.

Clearly, this hasn't been about me. It's been about God's desire to reveal Himself to those whom He loves. I would prefer to be a pain-free, boring bystander in all this, but that hasn't happened. Ten years from now, I hope all you remember is that there was a woman who asked you to pray for rain. You'll forget who the woman was, but you'll remember that you prayed in faith with your umbrellas open and waited for God to make it rain. And He did.

Since 2005, Linda has moved in and out of remission in ways that doctors can't fully explain. God has miraculously kept her alive far, far beyond what any medical professional would have predicted. But perhaps the greater miracles are in her soul. She has become a woman strong in faith and prayer, coupled with deep and peaceful surrender to whatever God chooses to do with her next.

PRAYING UNDER FIRE

Like Linda, we also saw spectacular answers to prayer as we prayed for Ian. Our praying was energized because we knew we were facing something evil and horrible. We rose to fight, with our friends right beside us. Cancer is a terrible symptom of a broken world, and I hate what it does (or attempts to do) to people. I've often wondered if flies and mosquitoes existed before the Fall. If they did, they must have had some good purpose, because God looked at *all* of His creation and called it "very good" (Genesis 1:31, NIV). But cancer was not part of His creation. I imagine Satan, like some mad scientist, cooking up cancer in his evil laboratory. But often, it blows up in his face.

Joni Eareckson Tada was seventeen when she dove into shallow water and broke her neck, leaving her a quadriplegic. As a young believer, she wondered if God had been looking the other way while Satan pushed her into the water. Forty years later, she now looks back and says, "God aborts devilish schemes to serve His own ends. God permits what He hates to accomplish that which He loves. Heaven and hell can participate in the exact same event, but for different reasons."[1]

Job experienced that confluence. Joseph was caught in that cross fire. He learned to say, "You meant evil against me, but God meant it for good" (Genesis 50:20, NASB). At the cross, Jesus found Himself at that same intersection. But while it was men who nailed Jesus to the cross, they were just doing what God had planned long ago (see Acts 2:23).

So what are we supposed to do with evil? Do we just lie down and let the Devil do whatever he wants, hoping God's got things under control? Of course not!

Two months into Ian's illness, I was in Mexico leading a consultation.

149

Ten minutes before I walked into my first meeting, Renee called to tell me that she was again in the hospital with Ian. He had been stricken with severe abdominal pain in the middle of the night. An hour or so later, my computer failed just minutes before my first presentation. As I walked into the meeting, a colleague pulled me aside and said, "This seems to me like a spiritual attack." Soon the whole group gathered around to lay hands on me and to lift Ian up in prayer.

So where did all that come from? Was it an attack from Satan?

Here's what I know: We live in a world that is broken and malfunctioning because of sin, like sand in our gas tank (see Romans 8:22). Sometimes our hardships are the results of what we ourselves have sown through how we live (see Galatians 6:7). Some sickness is God's supernatural judgment on specific sins (see Acts 12:23; 1 Corinthians 11:30). In some cases, Satan or his minions are directly involved (see Job 2:7). But no problem or sickness can touch us without God's permission. It's all Father filtered, and He sometimes allows such things so that *through* them we can see His glory and power (see John 9:1-3; Romans 8:28-29).

I don't know if Satan was specifically involved with Ian's pain or my computer failure. But Ephesians 6:10-18 makes it clear that our struggle is not against flesh and blood. It is normal for God's children to experience opposition from our enemy. In fact, if we are not experiencing opposition, we might want to take a hard look at our lives. We just may be on the sidelines of God's great purposes.

Since opposition is normal for us as believers, Paul told us what to do: Be strong, stand firm, and resist the Enemy. That is one of the big prayer lessons we've learned in the midst of our pain — extinguish the flaming arrows of doubt and fear. Don't believe the lies that Satan offers us when we are in pain. Instead, put on the armor of God, which is a full understanding of the Gospel and who we are in Christ.

PRAYING THROUGH THE MOGULS

Until now you have not asked for anything in my name. Ask and you will receive, and your joy will be complete. (John 16:24, NIV)

Praying in the face of pain is not a walk in the park. It's more like hopping moguls on a double black diamond ski slope — more excitement than most of us feel prepared to endure.

It turned out that the abdominal pain Ian experienced while I was in Mexico was caused by a gallstone, something often more painful than labor pains. Yet as the doctors discovered the gallstone, something wonderful began to be revealed. After the crisis, our oncologist asked the radiologist to carefully review the scan to determine the exact reduction of Ian's tumor. I'll never forget her response: "What tumor? I didn't see any tumor in there."

A few days later, I wrote this:

March 22, 2008

Thursday was the day of pain. Ian bravely endured the boring of two holes in his pelvic bone for bone marrow samples. I was there holding his hand, and I contributed to the procedure by passing out. I'll always remember Ian's hand dangling down from the operating table while I held his hand from the floor.

On Friday, I asked Ian how he'd like to celebrate his two days of relative health before resuming chemotherapy. The crazy idea of skiing came up, the doctor said okay, and we ran with it. A friend offered their ski-out condo. Another offered discount tickets. So, we were on our way!

Then, as we drove up through the mountains, we received a call from the oncologist with preliminary results of Ian's bone marrow tests. The last sample in early February contained 92 percent cancer cells. Now it shows 0 percent! Zip!

We'll see how Ian does with skiing. I remember him lying in bed at the hospital and the doctor talking about him walking around the block. At the time, that seemed so far out of reach. Now look at him.

This whole experience has been a bit like a ski slope, with drop-offs and moguls. And spectacular views of God's stunning handiwork.

So, you want to learn to pray? Sometimes God answers with moguls. Sometimes it's a marathon.

PRAYING WITHOUT LOSING HEART

Now He was telling them a parable to show that at all times they ought to pray and not to lose heart. (Luke 18:1, NASB)

In the days that followed our ski adventure, a more thorough analysis of the tests revealed that we had not yet reached the summit of being cancer free. It turned out that there were suspicious shadows on Ian's CT scan and negligible traces of cancer in his bone marrow. Like the pilgrim in Bunyan's *Pilgrim's Progress,* we looked ahead and saw a difficult road.

Throughout this ordeal I thought about others with a different story, those who weren't seeing their prayers answered the way they'd like. What about those others living with ongoing disabilities, losing battles with disease, or grieving the tragic death of a child? Did our progress raise hard questions for them? Did our joy deepen their pain? I wondered how I would be responding if things were going differently. Our feelings would be different, but our faith, I believed, would be the same.

Praying in the face of pain can be like an obstacle course; sometimes you end up facedown in the mud. The question is whether you'll get up again to press on. The day we received that ominous diagnosis of alveolar rhabdomyosarcoma, it felt like an emotional hemorrhage had broken loose in my brain. The look of grave concern on the face of the nurse practitioner was seared into my mind. I tried to continue caring for Ian, making phone calls, dealing with what was in front of me. And I called a dear friend to come. Within an hour he picked me up. I managed to close the passenger door before I began sobbing and wailing. I was facing the reality of death. After a while, the torrent slowed. I began to move on and to live with that reality. I did not give up. But the idea of Ian's death had been forced into my field of view, along with the range of possibilities that I was preparing to face, the options I was prepared to accept from the hand of God. And I was still convinced that God is good.

We were facing a road of persevering to eradicate the cancer and rebuild Ian's health. The drama of near death and miraculous progress was passing. The dust was clearing, yet the drudgery of pressing on through weakness and nausea and pain remained. Praying in the face of pain often requires endurance. So we pulled on our hiking boots and trudged on toward the summit we longed to see.

PRAYING THROUGH HARD DECISIONS

Pain can be disorienting, bewildering, like an unexpected two-by-four across the side of the head. Our prayers come out like a mere yelp, and it's hard to get much beyond that.

In the thick of things, sometimes my brain would freeze, like an overloaded computer. Sometimes I'd stand in the closet unable to decide what to wear, or wander around in the hospital cafeteria wondering what to eat. The simplest decisions were sometimes just too much. My mental and emotional bandwidth was occupied by the hardest decisions of my life. I longed for someone to step in and make the right decisions for us. It was an unwelcome opportunity to connect more deeply with Wisdom Himself.

The other day I was discussing a sticky issue with my boss when he said, "That's your call, David. You decide what to do." Something inside me groaned. It would be so much easier if he would make that decision for me! I wouldn't have to think and pray in the same way. But leaders make decisions, and he was spurring me to lead.

The questions we faced as Ian's parents seemed endless and terribly important. God had answered our prayers to the point where we were nearly certain he was cured. Should we continue the harsh course of treatment set before us, just in case? It seemed foolish not to. We needed clear direction from God and great courage to follow that direction.

As a leader, countless times I'd prayed for wisdom from above. Now, as a parent, I needed supernatural wisdom more than ever. My child's life was on the line! James 1:5 fit like a glove. After exhorting us to embrace trials as friends, James went on to say: "But if any of you lacks wisdom, let him ask of God, who gives to all generously and without reproach, and it will be given to him" (NASB). I realized that James's promise of wisdom was especially addressed to those of us in pain. So I prayed. Boy, did I pray!

In the meantime, one of Ian's best friends beat up one of his not-so-best friends for making fun of Ian's bald head. That's another approach.

PRAYING THROUGH OUR MOTIVES

Some of the wisdom needed in the midst of pain is insight into our own hearts and motives. Pain lays open our hearts like a surgeon. In 1 Corinthians 4:1-4 Paul made it clear that it's very hard for us to see our own motives clearly. In fact, Paul left it to God to sort that out for him. Nonetheless, pain does boil motives to the surface. So I found myself asking God if our motives were more like Hezekiah's or Paul's.

King Hezekiah had been greatly used by God. But when he faced death, it became clear that he was more obsessed with getting what he wanted than with God's grand purposes for his life.

In those days Hezekiah became ill and was at the point of death. The prophet Isaiah son of Amoz went to him and said, "This is what the LORD says: Put your house in order, because you are going to die; you will not recover."

Hezekiah turned his face to the wall and prayed to the LORD, "Remember, O LORD, how I have walked before you faithfully and with wholehearted devotion and have done what is good in your eyes." And Hezekiah wept bitterly. (Isaiah 38:1-3, NIV)

Contrast Hezekiah's attitude with the apostle Paul's:

For to me, to live is Christ and to die is gain. If I am to go on living in the body, this will mean fruitful labor for me. Yet what shall I choose? I do not know! I am torn between the two: I desire to depart and be with Christ, which is better by far; but it is more necessary for you that I remain in the body. Convinced of this, I know that I will remain, and I will continue with all of you for your progress and joy in the faith. (Philippians 1:21-25, NIV)

Hezekiah felt that God owed him a long life. He feared death because he thought it was "the pit of nothingness" (Isaiah 38:17, NASB). So when he faced death, he was desperate, clinging to life like he was dangling over the end of his existence. How sad! But our merciful God gave the king another fifteen years. It's interesting, though, to read the next chapter. In those extra fifteen years, Hezekiah unintentionally destroyed what God had built and preserved through him.

Paul, on the other hand, faced death again and again without fear, without self-pity. He did what was prudent to preserve his life, but he did not act out of selfishness. Rather, he preserved his life so that he could serve and bless others.

Why were we praying so hard to preserve Ian's life? Was it because we feared his death? No! It was because we believed God had noble purposes for Ian's life in the years ahead. And those purposes were already being fulfilled. People all over the world were being inspired by his courage and faith. Even the Olympic athletes we'd met at the hospital were inspired. Somehow they identified with the sacrifice and focus required of Ian to fight his battle. He spurred them on as they prepared for Beijing. And he spurred all of us on toward an even greater prize.

PRAYING FOR A MIRACLE

Pain pushes us to stop dinking around with small prayers. You don't ask for a pistol when you really need an army. You don't ask for a bicycle when you really need a truck. Extraordinary needs evoke extraordinary prayers. Besides, hanging out with Olympic athletes inspired us to think big thoughts. Instead of thinking something was too difficult, we began to think, *Why not?*

We've been taught to think big thoughts about God and to ask big things of God. A few months into Ian's battle with cancer, it seemed like we were on a roll, seeing miracles nearly once a week. So in the coming weeks, when I heard an announcement for a big youth conference, I thought, *Lord, would it be too much to ask that Ian would be able to fully participate in this conference?* Ian and his two brothers really wanted to go, and it seemed so timely for each of them. Ian wanted to go so badly that he said he'd be willing to just sit in the sound room and watch.

This was a big ask. Ian's previous two chemo treatments had left him with a dangerously low white blood cell count and a severely compromised immune system, requiring him to stay in isolation. What we were about to ask—for Ian's blood cell count to be high enough to join a room full of hundreds of people—wasn't as big as asking the sun to reverse its course (as God had done for Hezekiah), but it was the same idea: reversing natural phenomena. But in the spirit of "Why not?" we began to pray that God would miraculously strengthen Ian's immune system so he could fully participate in the conference.

A few days later, I wrote to friends:

> I'm sticking my neck out in prayer for Ian. I so want him to be able to go to the Desperation conference. Yet his count has dropped below the critical 500 level down to 200. And he was battling a low-grade fever last night. He seemed so frustrated when we discussed the implications if his counts don't rise today. Lord, will You answer our prayers and reverse this before his next blood test this afternoon? It would be such a blessing. And it would be such a disappointment if You don't. Once again, I call on You to pour health and healing into his body.

The very next day Ian's blood count rebounded beyond the minimum we were hoping for (500) and soared to 2,400! I imagine a chart of Ian's blood counts with skid marks at the bottom where it had been plummeting to zero but instead did a sudden reversal and raced back beyond 2,000. At this point, Ian's immune system was probably stronger than mine.

What kind of God does that? It was exciting to see Him reveal Himself like that—to us, to our friends, and to our neighbors who were all watching closely. Before all this pain, most of our neighbors were not interested in our faith. Now they were on the edge of their seats watching us pray, and even praying with us.

We all love miracles, but few of us want to live in the place where we need a miracle to succeed or survive. We'd rather watch from the audience. But sometimes God chooses us out of the crowd to join Him up on stage, where He intends to amaze everyone. "You there, in the green sweater. Come on up here." Not knowing what to expect, we stumble forward, just as curious as everyone else. No, *a lot more* curious than anyone else. And when it seems like only a miracle will do, we begin to pray as we've never prayed before.

PRAYING THROUGH ANXIETY

We had mountaintop moments in which we confidently stuck out our necks asking for miracles, but anxiety was no stranger to us during those times. We were filled with faith, but we were still human. Once again I had crawled out on a limb asking God for something so big—for Ian to go to the conference—and I was anxious out there. In desperation, I clung to Philippians 4:4-8 and waited for Him to show up.

Paul told the Philippians, "Rejoice in the Lord always; again I will say, rejoice!" (verse 4, NASB). Throughout that day, as we waited to hear the results of Ian's blood test, I tried to keep myself focused on the Master, just as Peter needed to keep his eyes on Jesus in the midst of a chaotic storm. The Lord is not anxious. He knows what is needed.

Then Paul said, "Let your gentle spirit be known to all men" (verse 5, NASB). Regardless of the situation—and in spite of my natural tendencies when I'm feeling anxious—I tried to avoid becoming harsh and forceful with the people around me. Instead, I asked God to fill me with His gentle Spirit so thoroughly that others would see Him and not me.

Paul continued by saying, "The Lord is near" (verse 5, NASB). I thought, *Ah! It's not up to me. I am counting on You to walk with me through this day, into and through each situation. I know that You can handle it all. I so readily try to take things into my own hands, especially when I feel responsible. I refuse to do that today. Please keep me strongly aware of Your powerful, loving, and peaceful presence.*

Then Paul got to the heart of it: "Be anxious for nothing, but in everything by prayer and supplication with thanksgiving let your requests be made known to God" (verse 6, NASB). So I prayed, *O Lord, help me to continually convert every shred of anxiety into prayer. You know the anxiety I am feeling on all fronts today. Right now I commit each front to You. I roll Ian's situation into Your hands. I trust You with him, his health, and what is best for him regarding this conference. Accomplish Your purposes today, however You choose."*

The passage also contains a wonderful promise: "And the peace of God, which surpasses all comprehension, will guard your hearts and your minds in Christ Jesus" (verse 7, NASB). *Oh, I need that!* I cried to the Lord. *Please make me an island of peace today. Rather, make me an overflowing fountain of peace. Others around me will need it, too. But it has to be Your peace. Whatever peace I might naturally bring is gone today. May Your peace surround me like a bodyguard, fending off every anxious thought.*

Finally, Paul exhorted us: "Whatever is true, whatever is honorable, whatever is right, whatever is pure, whatever is lovely, whatever is of good repute, if there is any excellence and if anything worthy of praise, dwell on these things" (verse 8, NASB). So I prayed, *Yes, I refuse the Enemy's whispered doubts and accusations. Help me to dwell on what it true, honorable, right, pure, lovely, good, excellent, and worthy of praise—which sounds like a description of You!*

Of course you feel anxious when you're in pain. Or when you're hurting over someone else's pain. The question is what you'll do with that anxiety. Paul urged us to convert every shred of anxiety into prayer.

Praying in the face of pain leads us into new spiritual territory, where we learn to pray under fire, to pray for miracles, to pray when we're worn out, to pray through our motives, to pray through our anxieties. Much of what happens through our praying happens *in* us. God uses prayer to change us. But most of what drives us in prayer is what we hope God will do in our circumstances. Will He say yes or will He say no?

WHEN GOD SAYS YES

As we continued to pray through the summer of 2008, the weeks brought one victory after another, including the doctor's amazing reversal about radiation and surgery that I described earlier. I described that *Yes!* to our friends this way:

August 12, 2008

God did it! CT scan: 100 percent cancer free! Bone marrow tests: 100 percent cancer free! Plans for surgery and radiation therapy: Reversed!

Thank you for praying. You play a part just as vital as the doctors and nurses. We use our hands. You use your knees.

So, how are we feeling? Ian threw his arms around his mom when he heard. Renee called me with tears of joy. Friends were literally jumping for joy. Ian ran around telling everyone at youth group tonight. And me? Well, I'm quietly reflective.

You see, today I had lunch with a colleague who has two sons. One is severely handicapped. The other one was recently killed in a tragic car accident. We cried together as he told me about how he felt when the police came pounding on his door to tell him.

Ian celebrating being cancer free

Why is God calling me to weep with those who weep as I rejoice with those who rejoice? I find myself remembering John Hersey's book *Hiroshima*. The main character was spared "accidentally" from being killed in the nuclear blast. As he ran into the city to find his family, he was confronted with hundreds of victims staggering out of the city, maimed and burned. It was so overwhelming that he began frantically running from person to person, apologizing that he was not hurt. Somehow that makes some sense to me right now.

Why me? Why not my colleague and his son? Why us? Why not them? Does God love us more than them? NO! He is writing a different love story with them. The angel Gabriel addressed Mary saying, "Hail! Favored one!" Did she feel favored as she watched her son being executed? Did Elizabeth feel favored when she heard that her son had been beheaded? God's favor doesn't always look the way we imagine.

And there is the heart of Amazing Grace. We tend to associate the phrase "Why me?" with being hit by tragedy. Instead, that should be our response to God's blessing.

As I look back, maybe God was preparing me. At that point, I did not know that within a few months the cancer would sneak into Ian's brain. The bell was about to sound as we were shoved back into the ring for another round of praying in the face of pain.

WHEN GOD SAYS NO

We finished out 2008 with a holiday season full of rejoicing, even as we pressed through hard chemotherapy. Then came 2009, which turned out to be a very different year. We prayed for miracles with the same faith, the same fervency, but Ian's health deteriorated before our eyes.

From David's Journal
April 24, 2009

Medicine has played its last card. It is very clear to everyone involved that Ian's healing is in God's hands alone.

We've seen God step in before. Even the most skeptical doctors acknowlege that Ian has never followed the norms. He keeps baffling them. With God's help, he's won every battle so far. He's undefeated and facing his toughest match.

Renee and I are deeply exhausted. Somehow tonight it feels like our emotional and spiritual support are wearing thin.

The image in my mind is that of a little girl sitting in the midst of a raging battle. Bombs explode and bullets whiz by, but she does not move. She's waiting. She's waiting for her dad, whom she knows will keep her safe. And we wait. We wait knowing that nothing will keep our Daddy from accomplishing what He intends. We know He will keep us safe. We're taking Him at His word.

April 26, 2009

We've been praying crazy faith prayers here. I feel like one of those pilots in a STAR WARS movie, strapped in for a life-or-death firefight. I engaged in the spiritual battle in earnest Saturday afternoon. At 11 that night Renee texted me from home to say good night, and I replied that it would be awhile before my head would hit the pillow. I was still stoked and going after it in prayer. But soon the Lord impressed on me that He gives to His beloved even in his sleep. So I slept until about 6 a.m., then resumed my part in this battle, while Ian carries on his.

Yesterday afternoon Renee and I had a profound time alone with Ian. He was alert and seemed to be "with" us. Tears were flowing as I said something like this:

Ian, I'm sure that somehow in the midst of all this Jesus is making Himself known to you in amazing and personal ways. And we want you to know that however HE is leading you, we want you to follow HIM. As far as we can understand His leading, we believe that He intends to heal you. But if He is clearly telling you that He wants you to leave us and go home to be with Him, then we want you to do that. I really mean that. Even though in the coming hours and days you'll hear us intensely battling for your healing in prayer, if Jesus Himself is calling you home, go for it. Don't worry about disappointing us. That would be very hard for us, but we'd be happy for you. However, if you hear Jesus calling you to fight, then I want you to FIGHT with all you have. I know this has been incredibly hard for you. But if Jesus is telling you to fight, then He will strengthen you. Don't lose heart, son. Just follow Jesus however He leads you. And He will enable you.

Then I strapped in for battle and kept at it for hours with a few breaks. Later, one of the dear nurses was marveling at Ian and said, "He is fighting so hard!" My heart rose with hope that Ian had heard his orders from Jesus and swelled with pride over my son's response.

I prayed fiercely. I prayed as I wanted others to pray for me. I prayed as we had prayed before, when we'd seen God do the miraculous again and again. But I was about to learn that praying is not always about getting the results we hope for. Sometimes God has something even bigger in mind.

QUESTIONS FOR REFLECTION

▶ How has your pain changed your prayer life?
▶ What are the best answers to prayer that you have experienced?
▶ What might it mean for you to "pray with your umbrella open" today?

CHAPTER 9

WHAT IF GOD SAYS NO?

I an's story did not turn out as we had hoped and expected. We were praying full steam when the tracks abruptly ended. Our souls screamed, "Noooo!" We, along with many others, had been deeply convinced that God was going to heal Ian. Ian's brother Calvin expressed what we all felt when he threw his arms around me in the hospital and cried, "It was not supposed to be this way!"

Ian's brothers as his pallbearers

Everything had changed. How were we to pray now? Turning back to Joni Eareckson Tada's story, before her accident she had prayed that God would draw her closer to Him. When she realized she was facing a lifetime as a quadriplegic, she said to a friend, "If this is the way that God treats His believers, He's never going to be trusted with another prayer again!"[1] Do you blame her? Have you ever felt that way?

PRAYING FOR YES, PREPARED FOR NO

Without specifically recognizing it, we had been prepared for this. In various ways we had often prayed, *Not my will, but Yours, Lord*. As I flipped back through my journal, I saw the underlying chord of submission was there all along.

February 22, 2009

> If God does not choose to intervene in Ian's situation with a miracle, it's likely he has four to eight weeks to live. So we are way, way out in the miracle zone here. Ian says we need a class 5 miracle for this class 5 hurricane. Humanly speaking, this could be described as a hopeless situation. But in God's economy what appears as hopeless may just be the prelude to a miracle. Still, we pray as Jesus prayed — *for God's will above all else.*

March 4, 2009

> No matter how many of us ask, no matter how earnest we are, God will never give us less than His best. Sometimes my kids used to put on a full-court press to get something they wanted. But if I knew it was not best, love kept me from capitulating to their demands. So we sit back and wait for what God has promised, His very best.

March 10, 2009

> You remember the stories Jesus told to show that at all times His disciples should pray and not lose heart? You remember how He told about a widow relentlessly bugging an unrighteous judge for mercy until she wore him down (Luke 18:1-8)? Do you remember how He told about the friend who wore down his neighbor with his requests for bread (Luke 11:5-8)? Well, there's an urgent mob

gathered outside God's window, and they're not going away. They're chanting, "Heal Ian!" Could God still say no? He would only do so if that was somehow better for us. No matter what God chooses to do, I will praise Him and lean into it.

Along the way, dear friends gently expressed concern about how far out on a limb we had gone in expressing our confidence that Ian would be healed. But we were not naive. Such circumstances strip us down to the essence of our faith—living in desperate dependence, crying out to the One who has all that we want, yet undergirded with profound trust and resilient love that will embrace whatever comes from His loving hand.

WHY BOTHER TO PRAY?

Linda also tried to prepare her praying friends for whatever God might do.

Since God has already laid out His plan for all of us, why bother to pray? What's the point?

Where's the power in prayer? If God has already decided whether or not I'll be healed from cancer, do our prayers make any difference? If God foreknows whether or not you'll get that new job or new house, why waste your time in prayer? I'm certain He doesn't hear our cry and say, "Oops, My bad. I'll do it your way."

God knows what His plans are, even if I don't. If given the chance, would I really want to alter what He has in mind for me? What if His plan is for me to die in ten months? Would I want to pray to convince Him to change His mind? Um, well . . . yeah.

But wait, what does He know that I don't know about eleven months from now? Well, everything. So, if I really believe He knows more than I do about what's best for me, do I still want to do it my way? I'm afraid so. We usually aren't satisfied with Him doing it

His way unless it matches our way, and I'm not so proud of that. I love it when it doesn't matter, when I simply say, "Okay, Lord, I'm in."

So why bother to pray? First, because God calls believers to pray and grow closer to Him (Romans 1:6). We do it because He tells us to. And second, we're not even capable of seeking God without Him calling us first (Romans 3:10-11). Therefore, when we pray with faith, it's because God has willed it and we have chosen it, so our prayers are a fulfillment of God's will. Both the sovereignty of God and the responsibility of man are all over the Scriptures, side by side. God knows what He's going to do, but He wants to hear from us.

If we're praying merely to satisfy our own desires, if we think we can give God answers He hadn't thought of, then we're not very wise. We'd risk denying who He is and expect Him to be merely our servant, not our Lord. However, if we pray according to the Holy Spirit's leading, then we are doing His will and trusting Him to answer perfectly, according to what He knows we need.

That's why I pray. Lately, I find that I spend more time thanking Him for what He's going to do rather than asking Him to do something.

We might think we know exactly what God's plans are, but we can't.

> As they approached the village to which they were going, Jesus acted as if he were going farther. But they urged him strongly, "Stay with us, for it is nearly evening; the day is almost over." So he went in to stay with them. (Luke 24:28-29, NIV)

Will He walk on down the road to the village, or turn and stay with us, as in Luke 24? Where is He leading us? Do we ask Him to change His mind and go our way? Like Jesus on that road with His disciples, God wants us to ask Him, urge Him, plead with Him to act, and if it is His will, He'll do it.

LEARNING FROM NO

While Linda has seen many miracles in her nine-year struggle with cancer, she's also seen the cancer return again and again, in spite of the many prayers that it would be gone forever.

From Linda's Journal
June 3, 2009

After nine years, I no longer ask, "Why?" Now I just ask, "What?" As in "What do You want me to do with what I know?" There have been many lessons learned, and I'm thankful for, well, most of them. Some lessons I think I'd prefer not to have learned, like how to do any worthwhile grocery shopping after three hours of nauseating chemo or how to survive chemo-induced constipation, a real pain in the butt. (Sorry.) Mostly, I hope I'm a better person for having survived all this. But is that where it ends? Is knowing things I didn't want to know all there is? I sure hope not.

I wouldn't have much to say about cancer if I'd been healed after the initial round of chemo. I did get better for a time, but the cancer never went away for good. As we say around here, "It is what it is; deal with it." My is is to have cancer for a long time, to live through and in spite of it, to not let it control any more of my life than it has to, and, it seems, to talk and write about it.

As a young woman, I wasn't known for my upbeat attitude. In fact, I was pretty melancholy, depressed, and grouchy. Life was all about me, yet I didn't like me or my life. The nos just kept piling up—and then I got cancer.

Thankfully, cancer teaches that life is not all about me. If I'd continued to focus on myself at the beginning of this journey, I would have gone crazy. How depressing to spend all my time thinking about a person with incurable cancer. I learned to look outward, to not focus on me. It didn't take much effort to see each day that someone somewhere was worse off than I was. I remember thinking, *If you focus on this disease and yourself, Linda, you won't make it.* Realizing that was a gift.

God honed me by allowing often unbearable pain to consume my days. It was the only way I'd agree to stop relying on ME. If I was only a little sick, I'd probably have kept on fighting my own battles, doing just well enough to think I could make it. But God allowed more than I could bear alone so I'd have to turn to Him for relief. "But when you are tempted, he will also provide a way out so that you can stand up under it" (1 Corinthians 10:13, NIV). As I gave into that, I became stronger than I ever could have been on my own.

How amazing is it that a self-centered, depressed woman finds out she's likely to die, turns around and praises God for the blessings He's given her through her illness, and shares her joy with others? How does that happen? Come on, you have to admit that's a miracle! God's main gift to me has been to force me to rely on Him for everything. And He had to take me down to do it. Thank God He did.

After all this time, I've heard no as much as I've heard yes from God. Funny thing, though; I've learned a whole lot more from no.

We can all learn more from no than from yes. We can also learn from how little children often respond to no. Our friend Leura walked closely with us through Ian's illness and death, and shared this surprising response from her young children:

My children were among those praying for Ian's healing, and they prayed with complete confidence that he would be healed. For them, it was a given. And then he died. I was worried about telling them—wondering if this would rock their faith and how I would answer their questions—but it turned out they took it so much better than I did. They didn't question it at all. It was like, "Oh, so Ian's in heaven? Well, good." The amazing thing about childlike faith is not only that you believe without doubt, but you accept no without questions. (Of course, they don't accept no from me with no questions, but with God, no problem.)

THE PORT IN MY STORM

No is uncomfortable. No is unsatisfying. No puts us in our place. We'd like to think that no will go away. We're like my teenage friend who said to his dad, "Please just say yes. I don't have time to wear you down!" But often God's no has a finality about it that requires submission. Linda is living that out even today.

From Linda's Journal
August 22, 2009

It doesn't take much to remind me that I'm still not there. ("There" being where I'm supposed to be.)

Sometimes I get pretty proud of myself. I go to Bible study, pray for friends' needs, and read the Bible a lot. I even enjoy it! I write newsletters and e-mails that people find inspirational. Sometimes I almost make myself gag at how close to becoming "holier than thou" I can get. Then I'm thrown back into reality, landing with a thud, still so very unholy.

Here's what knocked me off my pedestal this time. My friend Marcia is in remission from breast cancer (Praise God!) as I write this, and hopefully will never have a recurrence. She's been out of treatment for close to a year, and it looks good for a full recovery.

Our prayer group met at a friend's house a few days ago, and I thought, *Wow, Marcia looks great!* She told us she'd had her port removed a few days earlier, and everyone was so happy for her. Except me. I just sat there staring straight ahead. No one seemed to notice, but I was certain my face was ugly with bitterness and green with envy.

Having a port removed is not a casual procedure. If there is any thought of a future need for chemotherapy treatments, the port will not be removed. I'd say Marcia's doctors are confident she's done with cancer.

Eight years ago I had my first port removed, but I had to fight to get it done. I was warned it was virtually impossible that I'd be cancer free the rest of my life, and I'd only have to have

another port inserted later. But I was determined. Well, duh, that's exactly what happened. At least I got four port-free years, and the second port is far superior to the first. Still . . .

I know this funny lump on my clavicle is here to stay. Most of the

Linda, Marcia, and their prayer group

time, I don't notice or think about it anymore. But when I do, it's just a reminder of the "always" in my life. I'll always have cancer.

So I sat there by Marcia that morning grumbling to myself, thinking about poor little old me, barely thinking of Marcia, while everyone else was praising God. Left to myself, I'd have stayed in that ugly place. But I'm not on my own anymore. Help me now, God, I prayed. Then, without planning to, I looked at Marcia and was truly happy for her, able to forget myself because I was reminded I already have everything I need, and this port can stay as long as I need it. Like forever. I'm still alive against all odds. Should I really be complaining?

God has reasons for saying no to my wish, for not giving me a free pass on any of this. He doesn't have to be fair. I dare not ask for "fairness" because I really don't want Him to give me what I deserve! From now on I'll try to see my port as a reminder that God is in control of my life. Enjoy your freedom, Marcia.

Linda's no has gradually led her into years of miserable physical discomfort. Our no came more abruptly, with the finality of a coffin being lowered into the earth. But the months since Ian's death have been among the richest of our lives in terms of what we are learning. I'm not saying that makes Ian's death feel worth it. I don't think anything would feel that valuable to us. But like Linda, we're learning more from no than we've ever learned from yes.

WE CHOOSE MORE

It's no surprise that since Ian died, I've been reading the book of Job with fresh eyes. I feel the blows of his losses, which were far greater than my own. I empathize with the eloquent agony of his soul. I understand why his friends felt compelled to find some explainable, controllable reason for Job's suffering. Otherwise they might feel vulnerable to a similar calamity. I feel how much their accusations must have hurt him. I am all too familiar with Job's careening between noble thoughts and dark questions. And I'm getting some insight.

Job and his friends were wrestling with what and who God really is. Who would do such a thing to Job? What kind of God is He, really? As author James Bruce faced his own grief over losing his child, he commented on Job 42:1-5: "At first . . . we cannot square this with our God as we had imagined Him, as we had dreamed Him to be. The God we had, we lose. . . . And then begins the new endeavor of the soul, to learn to understand this real God."[2]

We have been thrust into facing who God really is. And it is frightening. The fear of God has taken on new meaning. As we give up our former impressions about Him and yield to what we now see, we can come out on the other side with a view of God that is either less or more than what we saw before.

We choose more.

We find ourselves walking into an unfamiliar place, where God is bigger and greater than we had imagined. We all want a God that we can control. Or do we? We all want a God who plays by our rules. Or do we? We all want a God who will never hurt us. Or do we? Do we really want a God who is just like us?

After Ian died, our sons Graham and Hudson were asking some deep questions about God over supper one night. Often the questions we ask at a time like this seek to reduce God to someone more like us, someone who lives within the time/space continuum that He created. He does not fit there any more than I fit into ten-year-old Graham's jeans. If all our questions could be answered neatly, all reality would have to fit within our puny ability to understand. Who would want that?

Samuel Rutherford wrote to a grieving mother, "I hope that your heart will yield. It is not safe to be pulling against the omnipotent Lord."[3] In similar circumstances, John Flavel wrote, "Is it right for children to contend and strive with their father?"[4]

I'll continue to gently ask my questions. And I feel the freedom to vent my feelings, as Job did. But I'll not strive against my Father. At least not too much or for too long.

When children are young, we expect them to obey, whether or not they understand. A five-year-old may not understand why he should not be playing in the driver's seat of the car when the keys are in the ignition. He just needs to obey. When our children get older, they demand more explanation. They want to understand why things are required of them. That's normal. But with God, we sometimes need to be more like the five-year-old. Otherwise our hearts grow hard and resistant when there are no answers we can comprehend.

TO WHOM SHALL WE GO?

Not long ago I was sitting in a worship service when the worship leader began sharing his experience of nearly losing his child to brain tumors. One moment I'm peacefully praising God. The next moment I'm caught in a maelstrom of anger and sadness. Why is his child now alive and well while mine is dead? My anger passed quickly, but the tears kept flowing. Friends around me were kind, and that helped, but it left me drained for the rest of the day.

I find comfort in Psalm 16 and John 6.

Although this psalm is generally upbeat and buoyant, the psalmist was obviously struggling, too. He began with a plea: "Preserve me, O God, for I take refuge in You" (NASB). That expresses where I am and where I want to be. I feel so fragile these days, so I have to turn to God as my refuge, my safe place. But is He safe? Yes and no. Yet as the psalmist said, "I have no good besides You" (verse 2, NASB).

I feel like Peter, who said, "To whom shall we go? You have words of eternal life" (John 6:68, NASB). Peter was responding to Jesus saying and doing some hard things that caused others to turn away. All the disciples were staggering. Some said, "This is a difficult statement; who can listen to it?" (verse 60, NASB). Others were grumbling so Jesus said, "Does this cause you to stumble? What then if you see the Son of Man ascending to where He was before?" (verses 61-62, NASB). It was like He was saying, "If you have trouble trusting Me now, you'll have even more trouble trusting Me when I reveal Myself more fully."

I'm with Peter. God has led us into a hard place, and I don't like it. It's painful and confusing here. I find myself perplexed, as Peter surely was. But, like Peter, I also refuse to turn away. Where else would I turn? Like Peter, I "have believed and have come to know that You are the Holy One of God" (verse 69, NASB). After years of walking with God in life and in the Scriptures, I've also come to know too much of Him to turn away now. I've come to know too much of God's love and wisdom and goodness. There is no better port in this storm. But I don't feel as safe here as I once did.

I feel like David back in Psalm 16. Although he was in a difficult time—so difficult that he was begging God to preserve his life—David also said, "The lines have fallen to me in pleasant places; indeed, my heritage is beautiful to me" (verse 6, NASB). I see that. I feel that. Life is not so much a journey through highs and lows, good and bad, as it is a walk along a path with two parallel tracks of hard things and good things. I would describe much of my life as hard but good. This past year has been a very rugged part of the path, with much pain and danger, but there also have been spectacular vistas and sweet fruit along the way.

We are now on a particularly dangerous part of the path. We are in danger of losing our way in unanswered questions or disillusionment. We need our Guide to take us by the hand and carry us over the rough spots.

> I have set the LORD continually before me;
> Because He is at my right hand, I will not be shaken.
> Therefore my heart is glad and my glory rejoices;
> My flesh also will dwell securely. . . .
> You will make known to me the path of life;
> In Your presence is fullness of joy;
> In Your right hand there are pleasures forever.
>   (Psalm 16:8-9,11, NASB)

I know of a man who years ago prayed earnestly that God would heal his leg. God said no, and his leg was subsequently amputated. That led to all kinds of hard questions for God. Today he says that God's answer was, "I am not going to answer your questions, but I am the answer that you need." That sounds a lot like God's response to Job. And to me—if I will listen.

THREE ROADS

I can't identify with the degree of Job's suffering. My suffering is distinctive and intense, but it pales compared to his. I don't identify with friends gathering to accuse me of bringing all this on myself. Our friends graciously keep telling us that we've walked well. And I don't identify with feeling God must have made a mistake. Okay, I've had that thought, but I've not sustained it with protracted arguments as Job did. But I *do* identify with having a disorienting head-on collision with who God really is. I do identify with being slapped in the face with how little I really understand.

John Claypool, the pastor I mentioned in the introduction, calls this slipping into the Mystery. Claypool had promises from God about his daughter's healing, coupled with deep submission to the Father's will. Like us he said, "I did not realize just how hopeful I really was until that afternoon as I knelt by her bed and saw her stop breathing."

In the aftermath of that collision, Claypool said, "I have looked down three alternative roads that seem to lead out of this darkness."[5] Two were dead ends: the road of unquestioning resignation and the road of demanding total intellectual understanding.

The third road was the road of gratitude. I'm trying to find my way down that road. Ian was loaned to us for thirteen wonderful years. Each week with him was a gift, right to the end. I am grateful that God gave us more than a year beyond what human medicine had to offer. I am grateful that in that year Ian became the young man I longed for him to become. I am grateful for the many ways that God flooded our lives with the love of friends and family. I am grateful for how our family has grown together through it all.

With less enthusiasm, I thank God for allowing this suffering in our lives. Linda says that she would not want to go back to her pre-cancer life, because cancer ushered her into a new way of living. She's ventured further down the road of gratitude than I have.

More than anything else, I am grateful for the fundamental assurance of the gospel, that Ian is with Jesus enjoying heaven. I miss him badly. It hurts, as it should. But now I have one foot in heaven. Part of me lives there now. And my life here is mysteriously tilting, or being set right, by that reality.

TURNING THE TABLES ON SATAN

Gratitude is the opposite of what Satan had in mind when he went after Job — or when he goes after any of us. He inflicts suffering, hoping that we'll curse God or at least withdraw from God and stop trusting Him. Here's a peek into my heart just three weeks after Ian's death:

From David's Journal
May 17, 2009

I did not sleep well last night. I kept waking through the night, and at 3 a.m. I had one of those epiphany moments that sometimes comes in those half-dreaming states. It was about avenging Ian's death.

Yesterday I offered to take Hudson to a movie to enjoy some time together. We ended up at the latest X-MEN movie about the origins of Wolverine. Wolverine is a tormented character who becomes obsessed with avenging the unjust death of the woman he loved. This gives a hint as to why I would be thinking about avenging Ian's death.

Does this seem like a strange thing to cross the mind of a Christian? Does it seem ungodly? Maybe so. But what occurred to me was Revelation 6:9-11, where we get a glimpse of what those who have died in Christ are doing in heaven today. They are praying about what's happening on earth! And they are saying, "How long, O Lord, holy and true, will You refrain from judging and avenging our blood?" (verse 10, NASB). I think it's safe to assume that their prayers arise from godly motives.

One of the well-known stages of grief is anger. Anger at whom? At God? Yes, at times we feel angry at God. He could have prevented Ian's death. Many of the psalms make it clear that God is okay with us expressing our anger to Him. But this morning my anger was directed toward the one who led the rebellion that messed up creation and introduced death into human experience: Satan himself.

I suddenly found some satisfaction in realizing that my life work of helping to advance the gospel of Jesus is, in a healthy sense, an act of revenge against the one who brought death into our family. He hoped that Ian's death would turn our hearts away from our heavenly Father. Just as with ancient Job, Satan hoped that the suffering and death he was given permission to inflict would lead us to curse God in our hearts. So this morning as we worshipped God, we defiantly stuck our finger in Satan's eye. Once again, death failed to accomplish what he had hoped.

Are there questions? Yes! Are we deeply troubled? Yes! Even Jesus Himself cried out in agony as He faced death, saying, "My God, My God, why have You forsaken Me?" (Matthew 27:46, NASB). If Jesus Himself screamed the hard questions, I guess it's okay for us to do so also. Yet that moment turned on Satan and became his biggest humiliation.

I'm finding satisfaction in imagining how frustrated Satan must be as he sees Ian's death deepening rather than destroying our trust in our Father, turning hearts toward God rather than away from Him. And I'm finding satisfaction in imagining how my life's work will in time help to seal Satan's ultimate failure.

So with Ian and others who have gone ahead of us into heaven, my soul cries out, *How long, Lord? How long until You avenge the wrongs done here on earth? How long until You return to make things right? How long until You set things back to the way they ought to be?*

Then I hear a whispered answer: "The Lord is not slow about His promise, as some count slowness, but is patient toward you, not wishing for any to perish but for all to come to repentance" (2 Peter 3:9, NASB). Vengeance will come. But in the meantime, God is patiently giving mankind time to come to repentance and reconciliation with Him. There will be more and more people joining Ian with Jesus, more and more people who love and trust the One who truly loves them, even when things are very hard to understand. How frustrated the Evil One must be.

I can almost hear him grinding his teeth now. Don't allow the Enemy to capitalize when God says no to you. Lean in. Draw near. Don't shrink back. This is how trust ripens.

STILL TRUSTING

Soon after Ian died, our daughter Nicole Lorelei flew off to Mozambique for the summer. My heart trembled as I watched her pass security to catch her plane. Why? This was not the first time I've watched my children head off on missions trips. But this was different.

My "little girl" was traveling by herself through Africa to unknown adventures. I'll never forget "losing" her in the Smithsonian museum years ago when she was about four. Somehow she had failed to get off the elevator with the rest of us. I panicked and ran around desperately praying, *God, protect my little girl!* But she's no longer my little girl. She's twenty-one now. And this is not her first missions trip. There was something else afoot in my trembling heart. I asked Renee, "Would you feel more comfortable if she were traveling with a man?" She shot back, "Of course!" Then I said to her (and to myself), "Well, who *is* traveling with her?" Of course I was referring to the Good Shepherd.

And there's the rub. We were probing raw and tender parts of our hearts. Would my heart still trust the Good Shepherd with my children? We entrusted Ian to Him, and He called us on it. He called in the loan. So as I watched Nicole confidently heading off to Mozambique, I heard Him whispering, "Do you still trust Me?"

I do trust Him. But it feels different now. Now, my trust is more completely stripped of the illusion that God will always cause things to work out the way I want them to be. I knew that before, at least in theory. But like Job, I now see God more clearly. I spend less time declaring what He is like and more time humbled before Him.

MISUNDERSTANDING GOD

Part of our apprehension to trust God again came not only from the disillusionment about God giving us a different ending than we expected, but also from how we misunderstood what He was telling us along the way. We had clearly heard from Him that He would heal Ian, that He would give him a long and fruitful life. We had stuck our necks out in faith, believing that was His promise to us and holding fast to it. Then we buried our son before his fourteenth birthday—not exactly the "long and fruitful" life we had envisioned. What do we do with that?

Did God really give us that promise? While some might doubt, we don't. Does it mean that God failed to keep His promise? That would be a contradiction of all that we know of God as He has revealed Himself in the Scriptures. We know that "God is not a man, that He should lie, nor a son of man, that He should repent; has He said, and will He not do it? Or has He spoken, and will He not make it good?" (Numbers 23:19, NASB).

Did we just misunderstand God? Yes, and we weren't the first. We fall in a long line of God's people who have misunderstood what God said:

- **Abraham** believed what God had promised meant that He would give the entire land of Palestine to Abraham's immediate physical sons and grandsons. But generations later, his descendants were still fighting for that land.
- **Joseph** and his father, Jacob, believed the supernatural dreams God had given to Joseph meant that he would replace Jacob as the family patriarch and ruler over Jacob's estate. Instead, he was sold into slavery and betrayed into prison. God was actually revealing that decades later Joseph would become ruler over Pharaoh's kingdom.
- **David** thought God had promised that His physical

descendents would rule Israel perpetually. After all, God had said to him, "Your house and your kingdom shall endure before Me forever; your throne shall be established forever" (2 Samuel 7:16, NASB). But David's descendants soon lost the throne. God was actually speaking to David about a descendant named Jesus who would come generations later and a kingdom that is still being established.

- **Isaiah** offered Ahaz a sign that one of his descendants would defeat the kings who were laying siege to Jerusalem. But we know that Isaiah's promise to Ahaz reached far beyond the immediate situation, for he said, "The Lord Himself will give you a sign: Behold a virgin will . . . bear a son, and she will call His name Immanuel" (Isaiah 7:14, NASB).

- **Israel** treasured many specific promises of a Messiah who would deliver them from oppression. They thought His promises pointed to a military conqueror who would rise from among them. Instead, they received a carpenter who spoke of a kingdom but left Caesar on his throne.

- **John the Baptist** believed the Promised One he had introduced to the world would deliver him from prison. Instead, he was beheaded.

- **Jesus' disciples** felt profoundly disillusioned as they saw their hoped-for Savior brutally executed before their eyes.

- **The Thessalonians** were so convinced Jesus would return any day that they were quitting their jobs and watching the sky. But Paul reproved them for their irresponsibility—and we're still watching the sky today.

- **Others** in the Bible "experienced mockings and scourgings, yes, also chains and imprisonment. They were stoned, they were sawn in two, they were tempted, they were put to death with the sword; they went about in sheepskins, in goatskins, being destitute, afflicted, ill-treated (men of whom the world was not worthy), wandering in deserts and mountains and caves and holes in the ground. And all these, having gained approval through their faith, *did not receive what was promised*, because God had provided something better for us, so that apart from us they would not be made perfect" (Hebrews 11:36-40, NASB, emphasis added).

Obviously, God's people have often misunderstood His promises. So where does that leave those of us who believed God would heal Ian in this life? How does that affect how we respond the next time God speaks? We are tempted to withdraw trust, to be more tentative in believing what God says. It's interesting that just before opening Hebrews 11, the writer quoted Habbakuk, saying, "My righteous one shall live by faith; and if he shrinks back, My soul has no pleasure in him" (Hebrews 10:38, NASB).

Our natural reluctance to trust God again could be compared to a boxer's reluctance to get back up after being knocked down. Once you've experienced real pain, it takes courage to get back up and face the possibility of getting hit again. Although we really don't want to be hurt again, we are determined to get back in the ring and to risk trusting God wherever He leads us. I sure don't have all the answers, but here are the thoughts I offered to my children as we decided our future steps of trust:

1. *Take this as an invitation to get to know God and His Word better.* R. C. Sproul said that any time he finds something in the Scriptures that he doesn't like, he takes that as an invitation to study it deeply because it indicates some dissonance between him and the God he loves. Among those who have walked this hard road with us, I am most concerned for those who know less of God and His Word. They don't have a larger context for understanding what is happening. Someone might observe Renee and I exchanging harsh words and conclude that we don't love one another, but they need to see that exchange in the context of our thirty-year love affair. In the same way, I

long for everyone who loved Ian to know God so well that they will respond by saying, "I still trust Him."

2. *Focus on obeying what you know rather than getting hung up on what you don't understand.* Moses wrote, "The secret things belong to the LORD our God, but the things revealed belong to us and to our sons forever, that we may observe all the words of this law" (Deuteronomy 29:29, NASB). Theological questions can be fascinating, but they can also become a cul-de-sac of useless wrangling about words and details that are beyond human understanding. Paul repeatedly warned young Timothy against such useless discussions. All my experience and God's Word tell me that I'll gain more understanding through obedience than through speculation: "He who has My commandments and keeps them is the one who loves Me; and he who loves Me will be loved by My Father, and I will love him and will disclose Myself to him" (John 14:21, NASB). If we focus on obeying what we know, we'll find answers to our questions along the road of obedience.

3. *Don't look for simple answers to your questions. Look for eternal perspective that helps you understand God and how He works.* When God speaks to us from outside of time and space, He sometimes has to answer our questions indirectly lest He mislead us. It's like a professor trying to explain quantum mechanics to a toddler. He's going to have to dumb down some things or it won't make any sense. As the teacher of my photography class was explaining the way a camera works, she said, "What I'm about to tell you is not technically accurate, but let me explain it in a way that you can understand." I see God doing that with us.

4. *God tells us that He is unfathomable—then tries to help us fathom the depths of who He is.* He tells us that His ways are inscrutable—then tries to help us scrutinize His ways. Paul told us that God's love is beyond our understanding—then prayed that we would understand God's love. I am fascinated by how often

Paul spoke of the mysteries of God. A mystery is the unanswered question that lures us into further investigation. Why do we try to reduce God to something that will fit into a thirty-minute documentary or a two-hundred-page textbook?

5. *Remember that God speaks from eternity, and His promises may transcend our conception of time and space.* Daniel was wrestling deeply with the plight of his fellow Israelites living in exile. So he sought God, and God spoke to him. But what God had to say to Daniel transcended his immediate situation and spanned thousands of years.

So why didn't God correct us when we were wholeheartedly believing that His promise meant He would heal Ian in this life?

"Why?" questions are often dead ends that attempt to reach beyond the limits of human understanding. Job's "Why?" questions led him to a painful encounter with the God who was and is much bigger than Job had imagined. I feel like God has led us to a place where we have to ask ourselves if we are willing to trust Him in spite of our unanswered questions. Do we want answers to our questions, or do we want to know God as He really is? What often happens at this juncture is that people force conclusions that reduce or distort God. Either they try to domesticate God or they secretly conclude that He's not worthy of our trust.

That doesn't mean we should avoid "Why?" questions. Such questions are enshrined throughout the Scriptures. God seems to embrace those questions and the sincere hearts behind them. If Jesus Himself asked the Father, "Why have You forsaken me?" surely it's okay for us to ask "Why?" on occasion.

I don't know why God did not correct our understanding. But I suspect that He knew it was better for us to live that way. Ian was surrounded by hope to the very end. We were not sitting around morbidly waiting for him to die. We prayed fiercely and loved him with our whole hearts until the very end. As we sat beside Ian's body, I said to Renee, "I have no regrets." I'm thankful for that gift. I don't know how this would have played out without those promises. I'll leave that with God and keep living by faith that risks loving and obeying without holding back.

Which leads to my final thought: I appealed to my children, and would appeal to anyone, not to let their questions hold them back from believing and obeying God. The author of Hebrews ended chapter 11 pointing to those who died seemingly tragic deaths while believing God. We call them martyrs. The word *martyr* is a transliteration of the Greek word for *witness*. They stand as witnesses pointing the way for us. In the very next verses, the beginning of chapter 12, the writer continued:

> Therefore, since we have so great a cloud of *witnesses* surrounding us, let us also lay aside every encumbrance and the sin which so easily entangles us, and let us run with endurance the race that is set before us, fixing our eyes on Jesus, the author and perfecter of faith, who for the joy set before Him endured the cross, despising the shame, and has sat down at the right hand of the throne of God. (verses 1-2, NASB, emphasis added)

Ian is not a martyr as we understand that word today. But he is part of that cloud of witnesses, cheering on his mom and me, his brothers and sisters to run the race set before us and to fix our eyes on the Author and Perfecter of *our faith*. He now knows the Author face-to-face. Ian now prays that we'll obey what we know rather than getting hung up on what we don't understand. He now cheers us on to believe and trust God with our whole heart so that we can fulfill our destiny as he and Jesus fulfilled theirs.

I hope we don't disappoint him.

PRAYING . . . AGAIN

Sometimes God says yes and sometimes God says no. We've experienced both in large and dramatic ways. God does intervene with miracles today.

We've seen that over and over again. We continue to see that. At other times He allows things to take a tragic course in spite of our praying. So where does that leave us? How do we pray with confidence now?

Paul faced the same dilemma. He had seen God do phenomenal miracles. Through and around him God healed many, and even raised some from the dead. But in at least one very personal and painful case, God said no to Paul. He would not heal Paul of his thorn in the flesh. So Paul kept asking, over and over. And I doubt his prayers were casual or half-hearted. The guy knew how to pray with authority. But still, God would not heal him.

I sense that God's response to Paul is also God's response to me: "My grace is sufficient for you, for power is perfected in weakness" (2 Corinthians 12:9, NASB). When I ask God to help me understand that kind of grace, I sense that He's saying something like this to me:

David, as you pray now, it's enough for you to know that I'm smiling on you with My favor. It's enough to know that I have everything under control, and that I have all the resources needed and will always use them to demonstrate My favor on you. It's enough to know that whatever I do in response to your praying, it will be a full and undiluted demonstration of My favor on you.

But, as you've seen, that does not mean that I'm always going to do what you want me to do. I often will do just what you ask. You've seen that. You've experienced that. You know that nothing is too difficult for Me, and that I love to do wonderful and spectacular things for you. I love to amaze you. I love to lavish My gifts on you. But there will also be times when larger purposes will prevail. There will be times when I say no to your desires in order to demonstrate My favor on you in ways that you won't fully understand. When I do that, My love for you is not diminished. When I say no to you, My favor on you has not receded. In fact, those hard times may be the times when My love for you is most evident.

Paul was so convinced of this that he learned to embrace those hard things, the times when God said no and allowed him to experience pain, weakness, insults, distresses, difficulties, and even persecution.

Jesus faced the same dilemma in Gethsemane. He had come to earth and set aside the independent exercise of His attributes as God. He depended fully on the Holy Spirit, and the Spirit demonstrated His miraculous power through Jesus over and over. Miracles were the norm around Jesus. When Jesus prayed, the lame walked, the blind saw, and the winds and waves obeyed. But when He came to His most painful juncture in the garden, the Father said no. Jesus earnestly cried out three times: "Abba! Father! All things are possible for You; remove this cup from Me" (Mark 14:36, NASB). Of all people, Jesus knew what His Father could do. Yet this time, the Father said no. And the Son returned to the foundational posture of His life: "Your will be done." He yielded and leaned into the painful choice His Father was making.

That's what we did in our house, as well. After Ian died and we got back into the full swing of our lives, we also tried to lean into our pain, to be mindful of not wasting it. But full swing is not full capacity. We tired more easily. Emotional margins were thinner. Ian was, and is, never far from our minds or conversations. We're walking with a limp.

One morning I went on a walk and prayed. I prayed for Linda and her son, Sam, as they faced some painful disappointments and challenges—or at least I tried to pray. Instinctively I began to appeal to God's compassion and sense of what would be good for them. But I was leaning on a part of my soul that had not fully healed, and I winced. That prayer path led to a dead end with Ian. I walk down that path with greater caution now. But I do walk it.

I know that God is compassionate and that He is committed to doing what is good for the people I love. But my ideas about good have been stunned. I thought of how Ian's death is like an amputation, like the violent deletion of Renee's fingers, cut off in a power saw when she was a little girl. I thought of how open nerves remain under her skin, and when she occasionally hits those nerves, the staggering pain can bring her to her knees. So she's careful with that hand, but she uses it all the time. And I'm careful as I pray, but I don't stop praying.

I imagine that in the midst of our pain, God listens even more closely. With seven children, we are not parents who jump at our children's every cry, but when Ian would whimper in even the slightest distress, we leaped to attention. When your child is in mortal danger, you tune in like never before. That's how I picture God responding to us during these painful days: "The LORD is near to the brokenhearted and saves those who are crushed in spirit" (Psalm 34:18, NASB).

> We're not just disheartened.
> We're brokenhearted.
> We're not just bruised.
> We're crushed.
> So God draws near, especially near.

And I keep praying, even though my prayers are not eloquent or loud. I imagine that God is weighing every sigh. Perhaps my sighs now have greater weight than entire days of prayer punctuated with earnest appeals. Perhaps. Regardless, I keep praying. I keep leaning in. I don't know what else to do. And I know it's what my Father wants.

QUESTIONS FOR REFLECTION

- ▶ When have you experienced God saying no to your prayers?
- ▶ How has that affected the way you pray today?
- ▶ Do you sense that you trust God more or less than you did before your pain?

CHAPTER 10

WHEN WILL
IT END?

E ndurance 101. Long Suffering 202. Perseverance 303.

You will not find these courses in a seminary catalog. You're not likely to even find them in your Sunday school curriculum. But these are requirements to living well, whether you aspire to be a great leader like Joseph or David, or a great parent, spouse, or friend. Peter wrote, "To this you were called, because Christ suffered for you, leaving you an example, that you should follow in his steps" (1 Peter 2:21, NIV).

Linda and I are not experts in suffering. We're still in the midst of our suffering, and we're still learning from it. But we have discovered five habits that have helped us keep going and keep growing even as we wonder when it will all end. These habits are honed and tested in the middle of the storm, as Linda described to an old friend in September 2007:

> This last round of chemo was as close to the 2000 torture regimen as I care to get. It was miserable. However, it still pales in comparison to that first round as far as pain is concerned. Either that, or I'm just used to pain and don't notice it anymore. (Um, I still notice.)
>
> My hands, feet, and mouth are the sorest areas. My feet and hands feel like they're embedded with broken glass and covered with

blisters. My mouth feels like it's full of canker sores. I haven't been able to take a hot bath or shower since January. No, I don't stink because I get to take cool showers. Wow, what a treat on a chilly autumn morning! Sometimes when Steve can tell my feet are really hurting, he will say, "Why don't you go soak in a ho—oh, never mind." I wish. The worst thing about not being able to touch anything hot? I haven't been able to do the dishes since January either. Now that's a real shame!

I haven't cut my hair, but it's only about three inches long. And there isn't much of it. It just keeps thinning and thinning, the longer ones falling out first. I feel ugly and have no idea what to do with it. Steve says I obsess on it, but I figure if I focus my irritation at losing my hair, then the other stuff seems less important.

But then there's this: I had a CT scan last week. The metastasized tumor that appeared last December didn't shrink; it just totally disappeared. It's another big surprise for my doctors, who didn't expect me to be here by now. But, you know, I never worry about dying. I just get sick of spending so much time at doctors' offices. And being totally exhausted. I still have to go through the last chemo of this regimen on October 8. I may have to be escorted at gunpoint; that's how badly I don't want to go—but I will. I always do.

It's a habit of mine.

HABIT #1: DO THE NEXT THING

There are times when "do the next thing" is all that you can do. Just keep putting one foot in front of the other. Just . . . keep . . . moving . . . forward. It's okay if that's all the strength you can muster, because that's all God requires of you at that moment. Jesus said, "So do not worry about tomorrow; for tomorrow will care for itself. Each day has enough trouble of its own" (Matthew 6:34, NASB).

It can be hard to do the next thing when you are *also* trying to control your life, protect those you love, answer all the hard questions, anticipate what might happen next, and guard yourself from more pain. It's tough running the universe. The good news is that's not our job. We just have to do the next thing God has given us.

Ian became a genius at this. He learned to do whatever was required and to live in the moment. In November 2008, he agreed to an interview with our local newspaper to promote a St. Baldrick's head-shaving event that would raise money for research into childhood cancer. Ian was a kid of few words, so there's just one quote from him in the article: "Take it one day at a time."

Ian learned to live in the moment. When we were preparing to celebrate his brother's birthday, Ian said, "Let's hurry. I want to eat before I get sick." He knew the chemo would make him sick by bedtime, so he wanted to enjoy life while he could. Later that week when I left for the office, he was miserably lying on the couch. But when I drove back into the neighborhood that evening, I saw him darting across the street, chasing one of his friends. Kids are resilient. We can all be resilient.

HABIT #2: LAMENT

It happened again today. I received yet another e-mail from someone marveling at my transparency in sharing our pain. I guess that I don't know how else to live. I long for people to be open and vulnerable with one another, too, and with God. Sometimes we think we need to pretend that life does not hurt. Sunday morning we dress up and paint on our smile. "How are you?" "Praise the Lord, I'm great!" We join what the band Casting Crowns calls "the stained glass masquerade." Then we go home and kick the dog and cry ourselves to sleep. We are not designed to live that way. We are designed to be authentic with one another—and with God. Otherwise, we shield ourselves from the love we so desperately need.

I love how real Linda is in this note to her friend:

Want to know the truth about me?
　　Today I have probably used the "F" word (in my stressed-out

head) ten times, yelled at Sam and Steve numerous times, thrown empty bottles across my parking lot, wanted to trash my entire shop, and whined about how much I hate my life. I hate having cancer. I hate being in pain. I hate not being able to do what I want to do (like work in my yard) because of pain, limited time, and weakness. I hate not having my hair, which was the only thing I liked about the way I look. I feel ugly. I'm fat, due to the bloating, and I have only one pair of pants that fits. I have been wearing them for three weeks! I'm sick of feeling uncomfortable in my own body. My stomach hurts. I can't stand up straight because of rib pain. I can't wear underwear (it rubs my skin raw), and I'm sick of being chafed by my pants. I can't even lie down to sleep because of my cracked ribs. Should I go on?

Steve and I are both sick, sick, sick of this life of uncertainty, pain, and weariness. He gives me way more than I could ever possibly give him, and there are days when his load in this just crushes him and the frustration spills out. After all, he has a full-time job, an elderly, needy mother to care for, and concerns of what he'll do if I'm not here to help guide our autistic son—let alone wondering how he'll cope if he has to watch me die. Sometimes I feel like he's sick of me (I wouldn't blame him), and I just want to crawl off and die anyway. Satan is trying to destroy what we've built and is using our pain and weariness to get to us. People say I'm strong. Ha. I'm pathetic. I'm running on empty now. If something doesn't change soon, I don't know how I'll continue.

Sigh. The venting is over. It kept me from bursting, so I feel better now. Thanks for listening. Just knowing you're there helps. It will be okay. Praise God from whom all blessings flow.

Do you have a friend you can be this real with? Can people be real with you? You'll never know unless you allow them to see you as you really are. In the meantime, maybe you could start with the One who already sees you as you really are.

THE COMPLAINT DEPARTMENT

Several years ago, I learned the value of writing psalms of complaint—
like Psalm 22, 42, 74, 88, and many others. Since God included them
in the Bible (plus the entire book of Lamentations, and the book of
Job), it's apparent that He embraces our complaints. Picture a father
enduring his son's wailing and beating against his father's chest until
he collapses into his father's warm embrace.

One afternoon soon after Ian fell into seizures, I spent hours in
some of the psalms of complaint and used some of those very words
from Scripture to compose my own psalm.

My Complaint

Listen to the prayer of one who lets God know just how bad it is
Listen to the pain in my cries. (Psalm 102:1, MSG)

Doubled up with pain, I call to God all the day long
No answer . . . nothing
I keep at it all night, tossing and turning
We know you were there for [others before us]
They cried for your help, and you gave it
Everyone shakes their head at me:
"Let's see how God handles this one . . ."
My heart is a blob of melted wax in my gut.
(Psalm 22:1-14, MSG)

Blinded by tears of pain and frustration
I call to you, God; all day I call. (Psalm 88:8-9, MSG)

My Appeal

Why do you hide your face and forget our misery?
Rise up and help us; redeem us because of your unfailing love.
(Psalm 44:1,24-26, NIV)

Do not hand over the life of your dove
Do not forget the lives of your afflicted forever
Remember your promises
[We are in] darkness
Rise up, O God, and defend your cause. (Psalm 74:19-23, NIV)

I'm standing my ground, God, shouting for help. (Psalm 88:13,
MSG)

My Affirmation

What I do, God, is wait for you, wait for my Lord, my
    God—you will answer!
I wait and pray so they won't laugh me off, won't smugly strut
    off when I stumble. (Psalm 38:15-16, MSG)

For he has not despised or disdained the suffering of the afflicted
    one;
He has not hidden his face from him but has listened to his cry
    for help. (Psalm 22:22-28, NIV)

Who, O God, is like you?
Though you have made me see troubles, many and bitter, you
    will restore my life again;
From the depths of the earth you will again bring me up.
You will increase my honor and comfort me once again.
    (Psalm 71:17-21, NIV)

By expressing our pain, we put it out there where we can receive the comfort we so desperately need. Otherwise, we're like a child who has been injured but won't let anyone touch the wound. We need to invite the Healer to touch our wound by dumping it at His feet as it is: bleeding, infected, raw.

Read the laments in the Bible. Let them prompt your own lament — your sadness, disappointment, and sense of loss. Let them coax out of you what needs to come out. God is listening.

HABIT #3: WORSHIP

I am like a grocery cart with one bad wheel that naturally tends to swerve off course. I constantly have to fight the tendency of my soul to swerve into some cul-de-sac of self-indulgence. Praise and thanksgiving help me stay on course, oriented toward truth. Some see corporate worship as group therapy or even self-delusion. I see it as telling ourselves the truth in a way that engages our voice, mind, emotions, and will. But I don't wait until I can get to church. I usually begin worshipping before I even pull back the covers.

Just two weeks after Ian's death, I wrote this to friends:

May 15, 2009

I find myself overwhelmed with grief at least once a day. And I imagine there will be more days when I get swamped in grief and will not be able to say I'm doing well at all. But most of the time, I'm experiencing comfort rising to meet the need. We used to live near the Chesapeake Bay, where fresh water meets the brine of the ocean. There is an ebb and flow. But somehow there is enough fresh water flowing into the bay to keep it fresh. I'm generally finding enough fresh water flowing into my soul to keep it fresh. Psalm 84 describes how that happens:

How lovely are Your dwelling places, O LORD of hosts!
My soul longed and even yearned for the courts of the LORD;

My heart and my flesh sing for joy to the living God.
The bird also has found a house,
And the swallow a nest for herself, where she may lay her
   young,
Even Your altars, O LORD of hosts,
My King and my God.
How blessed are those who dwell in Your house!
They are ever praising You. (verses 1-4, NASB)

Throughout our final weeks with Ian, whenever possible I would get to church on Sunday morning to worship together with others. One of our pastors said, "Worship your way through it." Ships sailing through storms need to constantly correct their course with a reference point beyond the storm. Truth is that reference point. In the midst of the storms of life, we get disoriented. We think good is bad and right is wrong and the One we should trust is not worthy of our trust. So we need to keep our eyes riveted on the gauges that tell us the truth. Worship does that for me.

There's another idea from Psalm 84 that captures my attention: "How blessed is the man whose strength is in You, in whose heart are the highways to Zion!" (verse 5, NASB).

I love the image of a "highway to Zion" in my heart. Whether or not we recognize them, we all have paths in our hearts. Some are self-destructive paths of anger or temporary pleasure or escape. But we need well-worn paths that take us to higher ground, paths that draw us into worship and transcend our circumstances.

Worship can help us take the next step when we cannot see the path. We constantly played worship music in Ian's room, for him and for ourselves. In the final weeks of his life, we saw that medicine had done all it could do. We could not see a path forward. I was talking with our family doctor and dear friend, who said, "When you can't see the path forward that just means . . . that you can't see the path forward. In

Indiana Jones and the Last Crusade, Indiana faced a canyon between him and the Holy Grail with no apparent way forward. He heard his father groaning behind him, and he believed that getting the Holy Grail was the only way to save him. Then he remembered his father's instructions, that he would have to take a leap of faith. So he stretched out his foot, stepping into the air. As his foot came down, he realized there was an invisible bridge. The way forward was there. He just couldn't see it."

That night I rented the movie and watched that scene. Just before Indiana found the path forward, someone said to him, "It's time to ask yourself what you believe." Of course, we weren't in a movie; this was real life — our son's life — but we, too, were being pressed to ask what we really believe. Songs of praise constantly lit our way and reminded us of the truth.

TWO RESPONSES TO HARDSHIP

Bad things will surely happen to us in this broken world. We can't control our circumstances, but our response *is* our "response-ability." Consider Moses and Isaiah:

- In Numbers 20, Moses lost perspective and got ticked off. He was fed up with the people blaming him for their hardships. God's response was severe: "Because you did not trust in me enough to honor me as holy in the sight of the Israelites, you will not bring this community into the land I give them" (verse 12, NIV). Moses died without seeing his vision fulfilled.
- In Isaiah 40, Isaiah gained perspective through worship. It looked like his people were about to be overrun by their enemies. Those around him were saying, "My way is hidden from the LORD, and the justice due me escapes the notice of my God" (verse 27, NASB). But Isaiah focused on his God rather than on his circumstances. He was enamored

rather than enmeshed. We can look at God through our circumstances, or look at our circumstances through God. Isaiah broke out into one of the most exalted worship songs ever sung: "Do you not know? Have you not heard? The Everlasting God, the LORD, the Creator of the ends of the earth does not become weary or tired. His understanding is inscrutable. He gives strength to the weary, and to him who lacks might he increases power. Though youths grow weary and tired, and vigorous young men stumble badly, yet those who wait for the LORD will gain new strength; they will mount up with wings like eagles, they will run and not get tired, they will walk and not become weary" (verses 28-31, NASB).

It's easy to get immersed in our pain. Worship gives perspective.

HABIT #4: CLING TO GOD'S PURPOSES

The latter part of 2008 was an endurance course for Ian. Tests showed that he was cancer free, but we knew that cancer might be lurking in places the tests could not see. So we soldiered on through months of intensive chemo according to normal protocols. One morning I wrote down some thoughts for Ian to help give him some perspective:

September 14, 2008

Dear Ian,

I imagine that there are times when you think, "It looks like I'm healed from cancer. So why do I have to endure more of this miserable chemotherapy?" And I imagine you remind yourself that we're doing this for a few more months to exterminate every last cancer cell, even those not seen by bone marrow tests.

But as I was spending time alone with God this morning, He reminded me of another benefit of a few more months of chemo. I was reading in Luke 6 about what happened right after Jesus chose

His twelve primary disciples. Rather than heading off to a leadership training program, they waded into a crowd of sick people who wanted to be touched and healed by Jesus. Somehow in the midst of that mob scene, Jesus turned to His disciples and said something like this: "I've called you to be learners. So learn from these people made desperate by sickness. Learn to embrace being desperately needy, because desperate needs can lead to real satisfaction with what is truly good and lead away from temporary satisfaction with cheap substitutes. Embrace pain, because it leads to real joy and away from regret."

That's my paraphrase of the beginning of Jesus' Sermon on the Mount. Check it out in Luke 6:12-26. He went on from there to explain the foundations of what it would mean for them to follow Him fully. Following Jesus often includes some unexpected and difficult turns. But it is the path to incredible joy and fulfillment.

Is God leading us to embrace being desperately needy, because desperate needs can lead to real satisfaction with what is truly good? Is He leading us away from temporary satisfaction with cheap substitutes? Is He leading us to embrace pain, because it leads to real joy and away from regret?

I know these may seem like awfully pious thoughts when you just want to get through each treatment and go play. But in the midst of nausea, weakness, interrupted nights, and fatigue, let's look for Jesus turning to us to say, "Here's what I want you to learn."

I was encouraging Ian to lift his eyes to the horizon of God's greater purposes. At age thirteen that was a lot for him to take in. But pain can spur you on to look for meaning. This is the big "Why?" question with a different spin. It's not saying to God, *How dare You!* It's saying, *Please show me more of what You are trying to accomplish now.*

I once heard Chuck Swindoll quote his mentor, Alan Redpath, saying, "When God wants to do an impossible task, He takes an impossible person and crushes him."[1] You may think, *Well, thank the Lord I'm no Chuck Swindoll. I don't think God has anything impossible to accomplish through me.* But you'd be wrong. When you submit to God, your destiny becomes greater than your capacity. It is beyond your natural capacity to love your spouse the way that he or she longs to be loved. It is beyond your natural capacity to be the parent that your children really need. It is beyond your natural capacity to be the witness that your co-workers need to see. Impossible tasks. An impossible person. So God chooses to crush us lest we fall short of our destiny.

TRAINING LIKE AN OLYMPIAN

In January 2009, Renee wrote on our blog, "Somehow, I think I had anticipated we could walk away from this and not have to look back. I am realizing that cancer is our reality that will be a part of Ian's life forever." She was realizing how those who survive cancer always live with the reality that it could return. Linda had learned to live with that reality—and its surprising benefits. She responded to Renee:

> This is one of those things that I kept to myself when you began this journey. How discouraging it would have been to hear, "Get used to it, guys. You and Ian will have this to deal with forever. Don't ever think it's over."
>
> But think of the Olympians. If they had to compete at their chosen sport without any practice or training, they would fail, or at best, do poorly. They have to go at it day after day for years to develop the strength and endurance required to succeed. The beginning can actually be the hardest part, when they're not sure they will make it. They have to learn what to do, what to expect, how to respond to weakness and pain. When they do, they can go on to victory. When the "pushing hard" becomes a habit, they know they can keep on doing it. So, like them, you and Ian are now trained to endure more than

you thought you could, more than most people ever will, and you are ready to handle what lies ahead. You've been trained in suffering and endurance. And your trust in God to care for you will be your true peace and freedom.

It's hard to persevere when you don't see tangible signs that your purpose is being accomplished. As the months of Ian's illness marched on, we kept anticipating relief from the strain of waiting and praying. When the cancer resurfaced in his brain, it was like rounding the last corner of the Marine Corps

Ian with the Olympic weightlifting team

Marathon and realizing that the last quarter mile is uphill. Think how often a football or basketball game completely changes in the last one or two minutes. Coaches will say, "Now we'll see what you're really made of!" And that's true. At that point it's no longer about training or talent. It's about what the players believe. So we watch teams either fall apart or do amazing things.

In the spring of 2009, it felt like we were at that point.

Faith is a muscle that grows through vigorous exercise, being pushed beyond comfort. And God is like our Olympic coach, fiercely committed to the purpose of building our faith.

You can be sure that if your pain is prolonged, one of God's purposes is to strengthen your faith. And He probably has other purposes that He will make clear to you. He may be purifying your hopes and dreams. He may be curing you of your illusions of immortality and indispensability. He may be bringing you to a point of surrender at which you are finally willing to let Him carry you. He may be pursuing all of these purposes at once or something different. Whatever purposes He reveals, cling to them and persevere like an Olympian in training.

HABIT #5: WATCH OVER YOUR HEART

> Watch over your heart with all diligence, for from it flow the springs of life. (Proverbs 4:23, NASB)

In the midst of our battle, a dear friend called from Britain to say that he and his wife were praying that we would not lose heart. He said that when we are praying for the same thing day after day, week after week, without seeing the ultimate fulfillment, we can keep mouthing the same words in spite of a subtle erosion of our faith. We can drift from believing what God said to merely "wishing" it would come to pass. He spoke of how he had seen that in some believers behind the Iron Curtain before it fell, praying yet not really believing. So when the curtain did fall, many were stunned. But it also revealed many believers who had become like refined gold.

We're learning that in the midst of pain, four virtues are produced like refined gold in a well-tended heart: hope, patience, courage, and surrender.

WATCH YOUR HOPE

We need to confront and resist erosion of the heart. Mark Twain once said, "Of all the things that I've ever lost, the one I miss the most is my mind." Even more serious may be to wake up and realize you've lost your heart. That's where I found myself on Easter 2009:

From David's Journal
April 12, 2009 (Resurrection Day)

> I expected to celebrate Jesus' resurrection today. And I did hope for some sort of "resurrection" for Ian. But I did not anticipate feeling so low that I would need a personal resurrection.

Yesterday was the fortieth day since Ian fell into seizures. It was the fortieth day since he'd spoken and run and played like other children. Coincidentally, those were the forty days of Lent. We thought it would be so poignant for him to leap out of bed yesterday so he could celebrate at church.

Instead it was another night with almost no sleep for Ian or those caring for him. And it was a day that began with vomiting up everything we'd just put into him. It was a day when Renee felt she could not leave him in the care of others, so the rest of us went to a church musical without her or Ian. Tears welled up

Renee caring for Ian at home

within me throughout the performance. As I watched Jesus' miracles portrayed, my heart cried out, "Why not my son? Why not today?"

The Easter sermon hit me in the heart: "The Resurrection Effect." It's a message that I've preached many times. But I needed to receive it in a new way. On Good Friday, the disciples struggled as they watched what they had hoped for seemingly slip away before their eyes. They struggled to believe what they had been told so clearly, but what seemed so impossible in view of what they were seeing. They needed a resurrection — not only of their hero Jesus, but also within their own souls. Hope was dying within them.

After Jesus was resurrected — after He ascended into heaven and they were left alone again, waiting huddled in the Upper Room — they received their own resurrection. Christ finally sent His holy and living Spirit to bring them to life. And the whole place was shaken. The whole city was shaken. Ultimately, the whole world was shaken. Hope had sprung back to life.

We need hope like a car needs a motor. When it dies, it's a serious problem. Dying hope is at the core of losing heart.

Viktor Frankl faced this firsthand as an inmate in a Nazi concentration camp, a place designed to exterminate hope. He observed how those around him were defined not by what happened to them but by how they chose to respond.[2] In the midst of some of the worst suffering in history, some rose above their circumstances by choosing to pay attention to what was happening in their souls. They watched over their hearts with all diligence, and from their hearts flowed springs of life in the face of death.

Some inmates had a wellspring of hope others did not possess: the hope of heaven. When we face death, that hope becomes more precious than ever. It's no longer just the sweet by and by. It's our next stop. And, like Linda, we find that hope—which is at the foundation of the gospel—to be a sturdy support.

From Linda's Journal
March 2009

As someone who has long had to face the likelihood of an early death, I often wonder why, as believers, we fight so hard to not go where we should be "dying" to go. When Paul wrote in 1 Corinthians about running to get the prize, just what do we think that prize is, if not heaven? Why do we so hate the thought of death if it takes us closer to God?

Please don't think it's cavalier of me to say I look forward to death. Actually, it would be more accurate to say I look forward to being in heaven, but not to leaving. I do long to live forever in paradise, but to do so, I have to leave those who love me, and I don't want to leave them. I'd be in heaven in perfect peace, but they'd be heartbroken. I don't want that.

I've given this a lot of thought. Cancer patients are obviously more inclined to think about death, even if we don't think we're dying. I understand now that looking forward to death isn't morbid; for Christians, it's joyful. It's one small gift that others can't relate to. The gift is in knowing where this all leads, and going ahead without fear.

So, why am I still here, when so many who are much younger and healthier have died? I've had to face my final months many times now, drugs and body failing me, cancer growing exponentially within me. Then inevitably I get pulled back from the brink and find myself in remission. And each time, I'm thankful. Why is that? Am I a hypocrite? Why do I look forward to being gone, yet praise God when He lets me stay? Does that make sense?

The longer I live, the more sense that makes. Such hope grows larger and larger through life and through pain.

WATCH YOUR PATIENCE

Patience is a tough one, especially when it comes to pain. We want it over. Now! But pain can take time to do its work. I guess that's why the Bible speaks of *long*-suffering. Impatience honks its horn and says, "God, have You checked Your watch? I think You're running late!" Patience quietly says, "God is always on time. He must know what He's doing." What does my impatience say about my real theology?

Luke 18:1-8 can be so perplexing. Jesus told His disciples the story of the impertinent widow "to show that at all times they ought to pray and not to lose heart" (verse 1, NASB). Then He gave the punch line: "Will not God bring about justice for His elect [chosen ones] who cry out to Him day and night, and will He delay long over them? I tell you that He will bring about justice for them quickly" (verses 7-8, NASB). Quickly? Then why do we find ourselves in the position of crying out to Him day and night? That implies a wait. The whole story implies a wait.

That got me thinking about this passage from 2 Peter:

But do not let this one fact escape your notice, beloved, that with the Lord one day is like a thousand years, and a thousand years like one day. The Lord is not slow about His promise, as some count slowness, but is patient toward you, not wishing for any to perish but for all to come to repentance. (3:8-9, NASB)

Peter was addressing those who doubted that Jesus would return, because it had been so long since He had gone back to heaven. Peter's audience was like the restless three-year-old in the back seat incessantly asking, "Are we there yet?" At that point it had been only about thirty-five years. And here we are two thousand years later. Peter said the Lord is not slow about His promise. He was surely speaking from the perspective of the Ancient of Days, the Eternal One.

Then I reread the whole chapter and noticed two things. Just as Mom and Dad *will* get the family to their destination in spite of the impatient complaining, God most certainly *will* keep His promise. And He often does it suddenly, when we're not expecting it. He does not always work that way, of course. But it's consistent with much of my experience with Him and much of what I see in the Scriptures. It's often wait, wait, not yet, wait, then BAM! God suddenly fulfills His promise. He sometimes reminds me of a martial artist—so patient, then springing into effective action at precisely the right moment.

That takes me back to 1 Kings 18. Israel had been waiting for rain for three years. We're familiar with waiting for rain because we live in Colorado, a high alpine desert. After three years without rain, we'd assume that global warming had dealt us a bad hand and it's time to close up shop. But God had deliberately stopped the rain to get Israel's attention. He was waiting for just the right moment; then He moved. And the rain came so suddenly and so hard that Ahab got stuck in the mud before he could get home.

So while we wait and while we pray, we're developing patience and tending our hearts.

WATCH YOUR COURAGE

I can be a wimp when it comes to pain. More than once I've passed out while giving blood or getting a shot. Then there's Renee, who has endured more surgeries than I can count. Everyone in our family knows the story of how I handled Renee's first C-section. The anesthesiologist talked me into looking over the curtain to see the baby come out. When I did, I thought, *My God, they've cut my wife in half!* I remember waking up on the floor outside the operating room with a gaggle of nurses giggling nearby—because there was another new father passed out right beside me.

It was the blood that always got to me. But I had to get over that in the first few weeks of Ian's illness. Because they could not get his bleeding to stop, he would often wake up in a bed soaked with blood. I learned to strengthen my buckling knees and find courage.

Courage grew in Ian like the stars coming out at night. Soon his favorite verse showed up on his Facebook page and remained there: "Therefore we do not lose heart, but though our outer man is decaying, yet our inner man is being renewed day by day" (2 Corinthians 4:16, NASB).

Courage became the hallmark of Ian's life. Have you ever wondered what they will say about your life at your funeral? Here's what I had to say about my son:

> Just before Ian was struck down with seizures at play rehearsal, a friend asked if he wanted to request prayer. Ian said, "No, I don't want to be known as the cancer kid." Ian would avoid drawing attention to himself, but the way he lived drew a lot of attention anyway. There was something about him beyond his winsome smile and quirky sense of humor. There was something inside him that was winning our hearts and changing us forever.
>
> Ian was tough. He was becoming a man's man. Last summer, we went on a father/son retreat. He went with

a port in his chest from weeks of intensive chemo that would have left most of us whining. He went with the "chemo cut," a bald head that marked him as the kid with cancer. But he covered it with a bandanna, hoping no one would notice. We broke into teams, and the one kid who had every excuse to be timid led the way with fierce enthusiasm. The final competition was a tug-of-war. Ian took the post position, tied in to lead the way with the rope around his chest. Mom would have begged him to be careful. But he threw himself into it so hard that the rope broke loose as his team won, leaving him splayed on the ground laughing. The kid with cancer not only fully participated, he led the way.

Just as muscles grow through heavy lifting, so courage should grow in the face of pain. I wonder what my children will say about me at my funeral. I wonder what they are thinking as they watch me face pain today.

WATCH YOUR NEED FOR CONTROL

Do you see surrender as a virtue to be cultivated, like hope, patience, and courage? We tend to associate surrender with white flags and losers. And that would be appropriate if we were surrendering to anyone but God Himself. But when we surrender to God, we are surrendering to the One who made us and is eager to display His beautiful life through us. This is so counterintuitive. When we are in pain, we naturally shift to self-preservation. We desperately want to seize control of the situation and make it stop. But that's not the instruction we receive from the Bible: "For whoever wishes to save his life will lose it; but whoever loses his life for My sake will find it" (Matthew 16:25, NASB).

Oswald Chambers took this enigmatic passage and made it vividly clear:

[God] rivets us with a pain that is terrific to one thing we never dreamed of, and for one radiant flashing moment we see what He is after, and we say—"Here am I, send me."

This call has nothing to do with personal sanctification, but with being made broken bread and poured-out wine. God can never make us wine if we object to the fingers He uses to crush us with. If God would only use His own fingers, and make me broken bread and poured-out wine in a special way! But when He uses someone whom we dislike, or some set of circumstances to which we said we would never submit, and makes those the crushers, we object. We must never choose the scene of our own martyrdom.[3]

Chambers makes me really uncomfortable when he adds:

If ever we are going to be made into wine, we will have to be crushed; you cannot drink grapes. Grapes become wine only when they have been squeezed.

I wonder what kind of finger and thumb God has been using to squeeze you, and you have been like a marble and escaped? You are not ripe yet, and if God had squeezed you, the wine would have been remarkably bitter. . . . Keep right with God and let Him do what He likes, and you will find that He is producing the kind of bread and wine that will benefit His other children.[4]

Psalm 46:10 says, "Cease striving and know that I am God" (NASB). The Hebrew word for "cease striving" means to "relax or abandon." It is the word for dropping the reins of your horse. That's a powerful image for me. I remember the first time I rode a horse. We gently ambled along until the last stretch. We were falling behind the group, so I spurred him on. Suddenly the illusion that I was in control of this one-thousand-pound beast vanished. I was hanging on for dear life.

But I imagine that in a race, the winning rider and horse experience a melding of their intentions as they both strain for the finish line. Which is in control? At that moment, it does not matter. They are one. And that's where we need to be. I believe that is what Jesus asked His Father on our behalf: "I have given them the glory that you gave me, that they may be one as we are one: I in them and you in me" (John 17:22-23, NIV).

In the midst of our most trying difficulties, Linda wrote this to us:

> Now read this statement carefully: You've taken the easy way out. Yes, instead of trying to go through this nightmare on your own, you've given it to God, who will carry you. Although not one moment of the past year has been in any way easy, imagine how much harder it would have been without God as your guide and helper. You have been able to rest in Him. Others who also trust in Him have helped to carry you through the toughest times. You have not been alone, and you never will be. And look at the miracles and blessings you have witnessed along the way!

When I exercise, there comes a time when I feel like quitting. My legs hurt. I'm having trouble getting enough oxygen. Nobody is watching; maybe I can just stop now. But then more noble thoughts come to me, goals that help me rise above my immediate feelings. So I keep doing what I've learned to do, putting one foot in front of another.

These habits of endurance have been like that for us. They keep us going. *Put one foot in front of the other*—Do the next thing. *Breathe*—Pour out your heart to God, both the pain and the praise. *Lift your chin and straighten your back*—Lift your eyes to the bigger picture of what God is doing. *Toss aside those thoughts of giving up*—Don't lose heart. Watch your hope, your patience, your courage. *And surrender control*. As you do, the life of Christ will flow through you in amazing ways.

QUESTIONS FOR REFLECTION

▶ What does it look like for you to just keep going today?

▶ How might you complete this statement: "My God, My God, why have You . . .?" (Then read Psalm 22.)

▶ How do you see one of our five habits of endurance growing in your life?

CHAPTER 11

GOT JOY?

Our hearts ache, but we always have joy. (2 Corinthians 6:10, NLT)

Are we just weird, or is it the rest of the world? An intensive care unit is not usually filled with laughter or singing. But ours often was. There were plenty of tears and agony, but over the years we learned from Linda that pain does not exclude laughter and joy. I remember the first time I went to visit Linda in the hospital after her original diagnosis, which seemed so hopeless. Linda and Steve have always cultivated a sharp wit, but somehow I did not expect that to survive the horror that had descended on them. As I left, I remember thinking, *That was weird. I didn't expect to be trading jokes today. But it felt good, very good.*

You don't have to let pain steal your joy—at least not for long.

FINDING GOD'S JOY

From David's Journal
March 13, 2008

Yesterday one of our pastors said, "Remember to find God's joy in this." I was talking to him from the hospital, and I guess he sensed my weariness. His words have been echoing through my heart as I search for that joy. This morning I went back to some familiar passages. What I found is not new, but it is fresh for me. My heart feels as if it's been plowed up. It doesn't feel good, but that freshly plowed ground is fertile soil for seed to grow. Here are some seeds freshly planted in my heart.

In the Bible, the word *joy* can refer to superficial feelings. But key passages point toward a joy that is deeper than happiness. Happiness depends on what happens. Joy can rise above what happens.

There is a joy that grows only in the fertile ground of hardship. I think that's what Jesus called "my joy." It's abundant and overflowing joy. It cannot be contained — not even by pain. Jesus spoke of having our joy made full and complete. It makes sense that if we experience His joy, it would overflow from our mere mortal hearts.

Have I got that joy? Paul "got" it in the midst of conflict and rejection (2 Corinthians 7:4). The Macedonians "got" it in the midst of poverty and suffering (2 Corinthians 8:2). The Hebrews "got" it in the midst of great injustice (Hebrews 10:34). Jesus "got" it as He faced the cross (Hebrews 12:2).

I confess I'm not there yet. I'm still in the oven. What can I do? Where can I find this kind of joy? Apparently I'll find it as I cling to the Word (John 15:11; 17:13), simply believe what God says (Romans 15:13), pray, and experience God answering my prayers (John 16:13).

What does it mean to "consider it all joy" (James 1:2, NASB)? I'm sure it's not pretending there is no agony or weariness. I'm sure it's not putting on a smiley face. It seems to be thoughtfully, by faith, entering into the way God sees things — the way they really are — rather than limiting ourselves to what we can see. It seems to be found in deliberately allowing God to wean me away from letting my feelings be controlled by circumstances. It seems to be found in consciously embracing the mysterious joy in God's heart (the joy of the Holy Spirit) even when I don't understand.

It's easy to miss joy when you are hurting. But as Nancy Guthrie said, after losing two children, "Joy was always peeking its way through the curtain of sorrow."[1] Similarly, in the days after watching his mother, wife, and daughter die in one tragic night, Jerry Sittser asked, "Is it possible to feel sorrow for the rest of our lives and yet to find joy at the same time?"[2] His answer and our answer is yes!

Pain actually can increase our capacity for joy. This thought first impressed me when I was a boy. Earlier I mentioned a book I read as a teenager. Author Kahlil Gibran wrote, "The deeper that sorrow carves into your being, the more joy you can contain."[3] I don't know why his words so impressed me that I've remembered them all these years. Maybe it was the first profound thought that my young mind had ever really taken on board. But it stuck, and I've found it to be true. When our lows are lower, our highs seem higher. Pain can boil life down to a few simple things, clearing the air so that what we had formerly taken for granted now becomes a source of joy. Deep sorrow can grow our ability to feel deeply.

Sittser wrote, "It is therefore not true that we become less through loss — unless we allow the loss to make us less, grinding our soul down until there is nothing left but an external self entirely under the control of circumstances."[4] He was grieving the pain of loss through death. But the same is true of all kinds of pain. We can allow it to grind us down, or we can allow it to increase our capacity for joy.

Is joy something we can choose? A friend often used to say to me, "Be encouraged!" And I would walk away wishing that he'd actually encouraged me rather than just jabbing me with that exhortation. Where's the joy switch in my soul? Where do I find joy when it seems so elusive? These questions have led me to search the Scriptures, which teach that joy is hidden where we can easily find it if we choose to.

FINDING JOY IN THANKFULNESS

Be joyful always; pray continually; give thanks in all circumstances, for this is God's will for you in Christ Jesus.
(1 Thessalonians 5:16-18, NIV)

I was sitting in a grief support group when a woman said fiercely, "I
don't have to give thanks for this!" And she was right. Paul told the
Thessalonians to give thanks *in* all circumstances, not for the circumstances themselves. In every circumstance there is *something* for which
to give thanks, and finding those things can change the weather in
your soul.

In 2006, Linda got the news she had dreaded. Her cancer was
back, and she was facing more chemo. But listen to her perspective:

> So, good news! My CA-125 count more than doubled to 135,
> so I have to start chemo again for an unspecified amount
> of time, up to a year. I know that doesn't sound good;
> it sounds horrid. But here's the thing: Dr. Boice made the
> decision for us; we didn't have to agonize over it. I have
> to make hundreds of decisions every day at work, and I'm
> tired of deciding things. Besides, I didn't want to have to
> choose to do chemo. However, it doesn't seem so bad if Dr.
> Boice tells me I have to do it. There's even more good news.
>
> The CT scan showed nothing. That means the tumor,
> although still there, is so tiny that it won't even show
> up on an X-ray. And the doc can't feel anything in my
> abdomen. Surgery is out of the question since there's no
> specific place to cut. Whew! He told me weeks ago that
> if my numbers went over 100, I'd have to take chemo, so
> I'm ready for that. He agreed not to use the same drug
> as last time; I'd refuse it anyway. That was like being
> run over by a train, then beaten for two hours with a

sledgehammer. Every week. For months. While bald. This newer drug has fewer side effects. It will make me tired (Will I even notice the difference?) but won't cause the deep pain, neuropathy, nausea, and hair loss as before.

So why is all this relatively bad news making me happy? Well, the injections will be only thirty minutes every week, instead of three to four hours like last time. I don't have to have more surgery. I get to have infusions close to home. I won't lose my hair. The pain will be less than last time. The side effects won't be as bad. The tumor is tiny. And so on. There, see? I told you it was good news. It just depends on how you look at it. And I'm looking at it as someone who has lived through much worse.

Here's a woman who just learned that what she dreaded for years has come upon her. Yet I count seven things she is rejoicing over. She is choosing to find joy in giving thanks.

That woman who growled, "I don't have to give thanks for this!" was right in a way, but she should take a closer look at the message of Ephesians 5:

> Be very careful, then, how you live — not as unwise but as wise, making the most of every opportunity, because the days are evil. Therefore do not be foolish, but understand what the Lord's will is. . . . Sing and make music in your heart to the Lord, *always giving thanks to God the Father for everything*, in the name of our Lord Jesus Christ. (verses 15-17,19-20, NIV, emphasis added)

The phrase "for everything" could be translated "over" or "above" everything. But every translation I've checked translates it "for everything." I don't think I'd say to that woman or anyone else in pain that they must thank God for the source of their pain. They might not be ready for that. But I remember one day when I was leading a discussion, I challenged the group to thank God for something they had never thanked Him for before.

I'll never forget a Taiwanese graduate student struggling to stand, who then leaned on his cane as he thanked God for the polio that had crippled him and left him an outcast in his own society. Choking back tears, he reviewed how God had used that hardship to draw him to Himself. He has never been the same since that day he chose to give thanks. Then a young woman stunned us by standing to thank God for being raped years before, in view of how God had ultimately changed her life through it. That's too heavy for me to comprehend. But it creates a lot of space for me to thank God for the sources of pain in my own life.

No matter how badly you're hurting, you can always find something to thank God for. When you do, you'll find that joy walks alongside thankfulness.

FINDING JOY IN YOUR FUTURE REWARD

Focusing on a future reward is a tough one for me. I like to focus on the ways God is changing my life *today*. Heaven seems so far away—or at least it did until Ian went on ahead of us. None of us is ready to volunteer for martyrdom so that we can go to the head of heaven's line. That may motivate delusional suicide bombers, but not us. However, when it becomes difficult to see any redeeming value in our suffering here on earth, heaven begins to look really, really good. Jesus said that persecution provides that kind of perspective.

> Blessed are you when people insult you, persecute you and falsely say all kinds of evil against you because of me. Rejoice and be glad, because *great is your reward* in heaven, for in the same way they persecuted the prophets who were before you. (Matthew 5:11-12, NIV, emphasis added)

Blessed? Really? Apparently so. The reward for those who suffer well will be *great*. It will be worth it all. I don't think that Jesus was pounding the pulpit and exaggerating when He said this. He was preparing His disciples for real pain that He knew they would face. And He held up their eternal reward as that which should prompt them to rejoice and be glad when they suffered for His sake.

Ours is not the pain of persecution, but the pain of grief and loss. What did Jesus have to say about this? He knew that His disciples would be deeply shaken when He went to the cross. He offered them hope that transcended what they were about to experience.

> I tell you the truth, you will weep and mourn while the world rejoices. You will grieve, but *your grief will turn to joy.* A woman giving birth to a child has pain because her time has come; but when her baby is born *she forgets the anguish because of her joy* that a child is born into the world. So with you: Now is your time of grief, but I will see you again and you will rejoice, and *no one will take away your joy.* In that day you will no longer ask me anything. I tell you the truth, my Father will give you whatever you ask in my name. Until now you have not asked for anything in my name. Ask and you will receive, and *your joy will be complete.* (John 16:20-24, NIV, emphasis added)

On the other side of whatever pain we face, there is joy that will eclipse it and even cause us to forget it. And that joy will never be taken away. Things may not be going our way today, but a day is coming when God Himself will give us whatever we ask. The pain of life here on earth will be a distant memory. With that in view, I can endure anything for a while.

FINDING JOY IN YOUR TRANSFORMATION

Do you ever exasperate yourself, wondering if you'll ever grow out of your irritating weaknesses? I do. I long to be a better man. I dream of being as good as some seem to think I am. On the other hand, I also hope that I can grow out of what others accuse me of being. I aspire. I hope. I pray. God is listening, and He takes me into His workshop. The tools there can be frightening. But in His hands those tools fix what is broken and create something beautiful.

The Devil may have intended your pain for evil, but God intends to make something good from it. Don't miss this. Treasure it. And give thanks when you see it.

NO LONGER AFRAID

I marvel at how God has used pain to make my beautiful sister even more beautiful. Just two months into her cancer, she could already see how God was using her pain for good.

> Ever since I was a little girl, I've been afraid of the dark, especially if it's behind me. The dark I left behind when I walked out of an unlit room, or the dark below as I lay on my bed, would make me uneasy. I'd scurry away as fast as I could, or pull the blankets tight around me, pretending in my mind that I wasn't really afraid.
>
> Last week I noticed that the dark wasn't bothering me as it once did. One night I was the last one to climb the stairs to bed and turn off the lights. Darkness swallowed up the rooms behind me. I paused halfway up and nearly laughed out loud. There was no urgency to hurry upstairs away from the fear. There was no need to turn and fearfully glance behind me. Instead, I thought, It's just a dark room. Big deal. Where was my fear?
>
> Instantly, the answer came to me. I already carry within me

something that can kill me. If I'm living day to day with a killer inside me, how scary could a little old dark room be? What could that room hold that would be scarier than cancer?

This cancer doesn't scare me, so why should anything else? This cancer, which is trying to kill me, has made me braver! What fear or danger could compare?

I also carry within me the one thing that can save me: Jesus. Now that is cool! The battle is over and won. This battle is between the cancer (evil) and the LORD, Jesus Christ. And we know who wins in the end. Even if I die—and we'll all die; life is terminal—I've still won. What's left to fear? Nothing.

NO LONGER DISCONTENT

When Linda's cancer appeared for the third time, she underwent a delicate surgery on a tumor that had metastasized at her liver. Waiting for potentially bad news from test results and looking at more chemo-therapy, you would think she would be depressed and discouraged. Instead, she found herself surprisingly content.

This morning at Bible study, I surprised myself by blurting out: "Whichever way this goes, I'm fine with it. Chemo or no chemo, I'm really fine with it." I wasn't just blowing smoke. As the words tumbled out, I was surprised to realize it was true. I was no longer dreading the test results, which would determine the next year of my life and beyond. It no longer mattered which way it went. If the numbers were low enough, I'd remain drug free. If they were high, I'd have to go back into miserable chemotherapy. I couldn't explain why I was suddenly fine with that; I just was. Then I remembered that my friends had been praying not only for the results, but for me to find peace, no matter the outcome.

I realized that because "In all things God works for the good of those who love him, who have been called according to his purpose" (Romans 8:28, NIV,) then if I loved Him, whatever the outcome, God would work it together for my own good. What a great, yet simple, realization! It was just a matter of believing the promise that good could still come out of this, even if the results seemed the worst they could be. This kind of confidence can't be faked; it's either there or it's not.

So, the test results came in this afternoon. Apparently the surgery was successful, and there will be no chemo for now. We're thrilled! For the first time in over a year, I feel free—and not just from cancer. I'm free to rest in God's peace, to no longer assume I must control my own life, which is uncontrollable anyway. Grasping that close to my heart, I know now that I truly can be at peace without so much as a clue to the future.

Someday my circumstance will change and test results won't be what we want, but when that day comes, I'll still be able to say, "I know what it is to be in need, and I know what it is to have plenty. I have learned the secret of being content in any and every situation, whether well fed or hungry, whether living in plenty or in want" (Philippians 4:12, NIV).

To go beyond mere acceptance and find myself in a place of joy—how great is that?

NO LONGER CONTROLLED BY PAIN

And now, as Linda experiences a new round of cancer and chemo even as we write this book, she continues to see transformation in her thinking and perspective. In August 2009, she wrote:

At first it was only for a day or so. Then it was two or three days. Eventually, it was four to five days, and now it never ends: the pain after chemo, the nausea, a consuming headache, weariness, and lethargy. Now they are constant companions that never go away. The side effects start off mild, then increase as time goes by, accumulating to the point of spilling over to the next round—850 out of the past 1,050 days of my life. I am completely worn out.

I usually say it's not that bad, and honestly, compared to much in my life (anyone's life, really), it's not. It's just the never-endingness of it that tires me so. Now every day is spent on my couch, reading, writing, listening to music, or sleeping. Wait a minute, that sounds like a lovely life—only without the pain, nausea, and inability to do otherwise, of course.

I learned a lesson at the beginning of this journey that I have to hold onto tightly: Live in today. For me, "today" is lying on my hammock, consumed by a pounding headache and waves of nausea that will not quit, too weak to move or even speak. Sam brings me an ice pack to put on my forehead, ginger ale with ice, and is now working nearby in my woodland garden. He hates the bugs, the dirt, the weeds, the resistant roots. He's off work today and wants to watch TV in his air-conditioned room. But he's doing this for me while I watch him work, because I can't do it and he can. That, and I pay well.

I look up at the blue sky through the canopy of shade trees, white clouds drifting by, so beautiful as I slowly sway in the breeze. As he digs, Sam quietly talks to me about ideas he has for making the drainage areas more efficient. My eyes are closed; I'm silent but listening. I love

Linda in her hammock

hearing him talk, love his newfound enthusiasm. The ice is soothing to my head. No thoughts of yesterday; no thoughts of what I have to endure tomorrow. Now I remember the lesson. I'm living in the moment. I love my son, and I'm happy. This is heaven.

Can you see why Linda says that she wouldn't want to go back to her pre-cancer life? She is finding joy in how God is transforming her. She is living out the teaching from these passages:

> Consider it pure joy, my brothers, whenever you face trials of many kinds, because you know that the testing of your faith develops perseverance. Perseverance must finish its work so that you may be mature and complete, not lacking anything. (James 1:2-4, NIV)

> In this you greatly rejoice, though now for a little while you may have had to suffer grief in all kinds of trials. These have come so that your faith—of greater worth than gold, which perishes even though refined by fire—may be proved genuine and may result in praise, glory and honor when Jesus Christ is revealed. (1 Peter 1:6-7, NIV)

Have you ever read these verses, shaken your head, and wondered, How *does anyone ever get there?* Some of the hardest Scripture to believe is that you can find true joy in the midst of suffering. *Because* of the suffering. Yet, these apostles (and Linda) all seem to agree. Even Job, amid all his ranting and raving, saw it: "But he knows the way that I take; when he has tested me, I will come forth as gold" (Job 23:10, NIV).

Pain brings transformation, and that's a cause for joy.

FINDING JOY IN HOW GOD IS USING YOU

I confess there are times when I get tired of hearing how others have been touched by our story. A big part of me says that I'd trade all the ways God has used our pain if we could skip Ian's suffering and death. I just want my son back, healthy and whole and here with me. But it's true that all of this has had deep transforming impact on many lives. I hope that continues. I want all this pain to have lasting value.

As I write, there have been 164,000 hits on Ian's CaringBridge weblog. There are 3,500 entries in the guestbook. Person after person after person has told us how walking with us through our pain has changed them forever. That means something. That matters. That's worth celebrating. In fact, I believe that we'll spend eternity hearing the cascading redemptive impact of our pain. That gives me joy now, and it will continue to give me joy throughout eternity.

Linda's experience in this parallels our own. For years, she took pride in having a brother (me) in "the ministry." She's only beginning to see more of the significance of her own ministry, how the ways that she's lived with pain have ministered to those around her:

> I don't want to sound trite, but don't you just love God? I take joy in the times He goes against what is "expected" and surprises us. This is truly an interesting adventure, and I won't say that I hate all of it. I love to see the way other people react to what's happening to me, that so many people I barely know have recommitted to Christ in their prayers over me. It's very humbling. It makes being bald seem pretty insignificant.

We may be unaware of most of the impact that we're having on others. Perhaps God protects us from seeing too much, lest we get puffed up or miss what He's trying to do *in* us more than *through* us. But the apostle Paul saw and deliberately leaned into how God was using his pain to impact others.

It is no coincidence that his "epistle of joy" was written to the Philippians from a prison. I know a young man sitting in a prison cell twenty hours a day right now. He is desperately miserable. The people around him are frightening. He's bored out of his mind. Hard to find much joy there, and I imagine Paul's prison was much worse. But from that place of misery, he wrote letters that continue to change lives thousands of years later.

He rejoiced that the testing of his faith strengthened the faith of others, that his life was being poured out like Jesus' life blood was poured out for others: "But even if I am being poured out like a drink offering on the sacrifice and service coming from your faith, I am glad and rejoice with all of you" (Philippians 2:17, NIV). Paul also rejoiced that his weakness helped others to grow strong: "For we rejoice when we ourselves are weak but you are strong; this we also pray for, that you be made complete" (2 Corinthians 13:9, NASB).

How often have you wished that God would use you to make a difference in this world? Does it give you joy when you get a few glimpses of Him using your pain for that very purpose?

FINDING JOY IN LAUGHTER

Ian playing Charades

Solomon wrote, "A joyful heart is good medicine, but a broken spirit dries up the bones" (Proverbs 17:22, NASB). The good old King James version says, "A merry heart doeth good like a medicine."

Scientists have confirmed that laughter is indeed good medicine. We used to live not far from the Gesundheit! Institute, the clinic created by the legendary physician Patch Adams, who believed in the healing power of humor. His was not a new idea. As early as the fourteenth century, a French surgeon named Henri de Mondeville prescribed jokes to help his patients recover.[5] Norman Cousins wrote *Anatomy of an Illness as Perceived by the Patient*, in which he detailed his recovery from an "incurable" illness primarily through watching funny movies.[6] Laughter increases production of endorphins, which are natural pain killers. (I wonder what endorphins look like. They sound fun.) Laughter improves blood pressure and circulation. Cousins called laughter "internal jogging." So we invited friends to send their favorite jokes to Ian, and they lit up our days.

Laughter is also a sign that joy is alive. Pain may have its grip on us, but laughter shows that it has not squeezed the life out of us. Laughter removes some of the sting of pain, like a cool poultice. Laughter relieves pressure and puts pain in its place. Laughter shows that pain is not in charge. And it can come at the oddest moments. Nancy Guthrie was leaning over the crib where her child had died earlier that day when her husband made her laugh. Through her tears she retorted, "How dare you make me laugh today?!"[7] Her joy was still alive.

Cancer patients face not only a life-threatening illness but the horrors of treating it. At these, they must also be able to laugh, as both Linda and Ian discovered. Both repeatedly lost their hair through chemotherapy. For both of them, their first "chemo cut" was traumatic, but they learned to laugh their way through it. During her first round of chemo, Linda wrote:

I was warned that my hair would fall out about twenty-one days after the start of the chemo treatments. We were concerned that Sam, eleven, would be upset by my bald head, so we decided to joke about it to get him prepared. We had learned to make light of so many things that otherwise would upset him. A middle-school kid, even an autistic one, doesn't need the embarrassment of a weird-looking mom.

One day in the car, I looked back at him and said, "Watch out! You might be sitting behind me when my hair falls out, and it'll fly out my window, back through yours, and hit you in the face." He seemed to think that was pretty funny.

The following Sunday at church, a man stopped to talk to him. Sam told him, "You'd better not walk behind my mom on a windy day next week. Her hair's going to fly off her head and smack you in the face." He wasn't smiling or kidding. I thought poor Al might have a shock-induced heart attack as I tried to stifle my own laughter. I sometimes forget that Sam takes things literally.

As the days passed, my hair started to take up residence around the house. As I climbed out of the hair-covered shower on the twenty-first morning, I knew the day had come. Determined not to be a wimp about it, I began throwing clumps in the trash can and chopping the remaining hair as close to the scalp as I could.

As I sat with scissors in hand, looking at my ravaged head, I began to cry. I felt ashamed and disgraced, though I didn't know why. Steve came into the room and saw what I'd done. Taking the scissors from my hand, slowly, gently, without a word, he cut off the rest of the hair we both loved. He finished the job by shaving the stubble until I was completely bald. Taking my face into his hands and turning it toward his own, he said, "You're still beautiful," and from that moment, I felt I was.

Now, many years later, it's a family joke that Mom's hair has become the other entity in the house. It's grown back and fallen out, all over the place, too many times to count. Some days, I hate it. Most others, it's just something to laugh about, as the guys pull my hair out of their freshly laundered socks and their salads, while marveling that I could have any hair left at all.

Our brother-in-law Charlie wrote to Linda:

Look, take it from someone who knows, bald is great. You don't have to get up every morning and take time to fix your hair. You save a lot of money on shampoo and other hair-improvement junk. There's no such thing as a bad hair day. I'm sure you have heard the term "hairpiece." Well it's really true. Not having that stuff on top to worry about brings a sense of inner calm. Being hair-challenged is not a bad thing. Welcome to our club. Dues are payable the first of each month.

Ian also cultivated a few tart responses to kids who would ask what happened to his hair:

- "The wind just blew it out."
- "I sold it."
- "Bad genes; my mother is bald."
- "I traded it for this body."
- "I was having a makeover and ran out of money."
- "See what happens when you don't eat your vegetables?"
- "Anyone who wears hair during the daytime is overdressed."

Linda's port was another source of pain and annoyance. When her cancer returned, she fought for weeks to avoid having another one installed for the next round. But someone found a great way to help her to cope:

> The surgeon was well aware of how much I didn't want to have this done again. At the hospital, he was very kind and did all he could to assure me it would be fine. This morning at home I removed the outer bandages and gasped with laughter when I saw the little purple smiley face he'd drawn on the wound. In permanent ink! Any thoughts of another ugly scar were totally wiped away. I couldn't stop laughing. That little face cheered me for almost two weeks.

If you make fun of that which is causing you pain, you cut it down to size and make it more manageable. Late-night comedians do it with our presidents. We do it with our pain.

FINDING JOY IN CHRIST'S JOY

Sometimes it's impossible to find the slightest bit of joy inside yourself. At such times, look for Jesus inside you. If He's living in you, then you've got *His* joy inside you, and His joy is unlike anything we can experience on our own. Nancy Guthrie said, "The truth is, a person can't just decide to have joy. Genuine joy is not an act of willpower or positive thinking. It is a spontaneous, soul-level response to the most solid, satisfying joy in the universe."[8] That's what Jesus had in mind when He said:

> These things I have spoken to you so that *My joy* may be in you, and that your joy may be made full. (John 15:11, NASB, emphasis added)

> But now I come to You; and these things I speak in the world so that they may have *My joy* made full in themselves. (John 17:13, NASB, emphasis added)

What kind of joy does God Himself experience? What is it like when He allows us to experience His joy welling up inside us? Maybe it's a little like the infectious laughter of children, which makes us smile and laugh with them. Maybe it's a little like that person who lights up the room when she arrives at the party. Whatever it's like, I want it. And apparently the disciples got it, eventually. "And the disciples were continually filled with joy and with the Holy Spirit" (Acts 13:52, NASB). Jesus promised to send His Spirit after He went to heaven. His Spirit is, among other things, full of joy. That's why when we are filled with the Spirit, joy flows.

If that's what welled up in the hearts of the disciples as they were being kicked out of town, I wonder what they felt when things were going smoothly. I wonder if this kind of joy can actually be greater in the tough times.

Joy is a fruit of the Spirit, and fruit is an overflow of the life of a plant. Trees bear fruit in order to reproduce after their kind. We used to have an orchard, and I can assure you that fruit trees don't grunt and sweat in an effort to bear fruit. Fruit just naturally grows from a well-cultivated tree. Even distressed trees often bear even more fruit for a season. I suppose God made them that way so they'd be sure to leave something good behind if they die from the distress.

This all can seem so nebulous and ethereal, especially when you're in pain. But here's something more tangible. Jesus spoke of entering into the joy of your Master (see Matthew 25:21). Your Master is living inside you, and He is full of joy. And He's full of joy over *you*.

> On that day they will say to Jerusalem,
>> "Do not fear, O Zion;
>> do not let your hands hang limp.
> The LORD your God is with you,
>> he is mighty to save.
> He will take great delight in you,
>> he will quiet you with his love,
>> he will rejoice over you with singing."
>> (Zephaniah 3:16-17, NIV)

Your hands may hang limp at your side. You may feel overwhelmed with sorrows. But in the midst of that, there is One rejoicing over you. He's rejoicing because He sees beyond the walls of your circumstances to a great future. He's rejoicing because He's so proud of how you are enduring. He's rejoicing because He's pleased with the good work He's doing in you and through you. He's so full of joy that He's singing. Think about that: The One who spoke the world into existence actually breaks out into song over you!

Got joy? You may not feel like you do, but it's within reach. You can find it as you thank God for what you had not appreciated before. You can find it as you think about that big fat reward waiting for you on the other side. You can find it when you notice all the transformation He's doing in you. You can find it when God gives you glimpses of how you are impacting others. You can laugh, no matter how bad things get. And when you can't find joy within yourself, no matter what you do, you can enter into the joy of your Master. You really can.

QUESTIONS FOR REFLECTION

- ▶ Where are you finding joy these days?
- ▶ Of the six ways in which to find joy listed in this chapter, which will you focus on this week?
- ▶ When was the last time you had a good laugh, or at least a big grin?

CHAPTER 12

THE FELLOWSHIP
OF SUFFERING

M ost people who write books about their pain are looking at it in the rearview mirror, years after their suffering has passed and they've had time to make more sense of it. So why in the world am I sitting here writing this book just six months after Ian died? Why is Linda writing from the front lines of her own battle? While we were working on the chapter on joy, she found out her cancer had returned yet again. (She has since found out that her prognosis is good enough to avoid chemo for several more months.) So why are we doing this? The simple answer is this: We don't want to waste our pain.

We are passionate about passing on what God has been doing in us. This final chapter is designed to help you help others who are in pain. They may be suffering physically as Linda is. They may be suffering emotionally as we have been with Ian's cancer and death. Regardless of what their pain looks like, there are people around you who need the comfort that has been entrusted to you.

The first chapter of 2 Corinthians describes well what we have been living throughout our battles with cancer. We are not experts on comfort; we're just sharing our lives. But our life experience is consistent with what Paul said in this chapter.

1. EMBRACE THE TENDERHEARTEDNESS OF GOD

> Praise be to the God and Father of our Lord Jesus Christ, the
> Father of compassion and the God of all comfort. (2 Corinthians
> 1:3, NIV)

There are people known for their tender hearts. I am not naturally one of them. In premarital counseling, Renee and I took a personality test that exposed what we both knew: We are opposites in many ways. Renee is verbally expressive, while I am reserved. Renee anticipates emotionally, while I feel things later, if at all. Renee is beautiful, while I am . . . less so. Most important, Renee is tenderhearted, while I tend to be indifferent. I was one of those guys who might run over a squirrel on the road and never look back. So it will come as no surprise that within a couple of years after marriage, we were growing apart emotionally. At one point Renee said to me, "You don't need me. If I was gone, you would just go on with your life and hardly miss a beat." I'm ashamed to say that although I protested her accusation, in my heart I thought, *You're right.* In truth, we were careening toward divorce. But God intervened through godly friends and mentors and through His Word. I'll never

David and Renee

forget the day it dawned on me what an emotional cripple I was and that I desperately needed my tenderhearted wife to help me become more like my tenderhearted God.

I think that Paul was naturally more like me than Renee. Remember how he was tracking down Christians to exterminate them? But God broke through, and by the time Paul wrote 2 Corinthians, he had come to know God as the Father of compassion, the God of all comfort. He had come to embrace the tender heart of God. In *Lament for a Son,* Nicholas Wolterstorff wrote, "It is said of

God that no one can behold his face and live. I always thought this meant that no one could see his splendor and live. A friend said perhaps it meant that no one could see his sorrow and live. Or perhaps his sorrow is splendor."[1] That's something to think about. But I am certain that we don't really know God until we know His tender heart.

FINDING GOD'S HEART

As we all struggled to deal with Ian's initial cancer diagnosis, my oldest son, Wesley, turned to his Aunt Linda for perspective. She explained that in the midst of her own anguish, she discovered the tender heart of God, who Himself had to watch His own Son endure torture and death on a cross. God could identify with her own broken heart.

> Dear Wes,
>
> My initial pain took me down to the bare nothing. With no hope of recovery, I got to the place where I had only God. Then I was able to realize that when it seemed I had the least in my life, I actually had the most one could ever have.
>
> You're doing exactly what God wants, Wes. Talk to Him, trust Him, give Ian to Him. Allow your heart to be broken. Then you will know more about the heart of God. I remember literally lying flat on the floor and sobbing that it truly didn't matter if I died, as long as I was with Him. Strange as it sounds, it felt as though I was lying at the cross of Jesus, and then I was free.

HE WAS THERE

Where is God in the most painful moments in our lives? Was He absent when cancer invaded Linda's body? Did He check out the day Ian died?

Years ago, I went to a seminar that featured prayer as a primary path toward healing. We explored the sources of our destructive thoughts and feelings and asked God to lead us back to where we first learned those patterns. In spite of my doubts about the process, I asked God to take me back to one traumatic experience that had shaped me.

As a boy I had just two friends: two brothers who were the only children within miles. One day they invited me to meet them on a nearby hill after dark. When I arrived, there was another boy who was much bigger than any of us. Before I knew it, he was on top of me pounding me to a bloody mess while my "friends" stood by and laughed. They had paid him to beat me up as revenge for some perceived wrong. I had been violently betrayed by my only friends.

In the seminar, I was prompted to ask God, "Where were You that night?" That question led me into one of my most profound encounters with Him. He showed me where He had been. He had been right there with me and even in me. He was there *feeling every blow* as that boy hit me.

And He was right there when a little girl I know was tortured and raped. He was there when Jerry Sittser's mother and wife and daughter were killed by a drunk driver. And both that little girl (who is now an adult) and Jerry Sittser would tell you that somehow knowing God was there with His arms wrapped around them in their pain has brought profound healing.

He was there the morning my son died. When Ian's vital signs were vanishing, all the medical staff left the room so that Renee and I could be alone with him. We sat on either side of him, each holding his hand. But the Father of compassion was holding *us*. The God of all comfort wept with us.

He was there with us, just as He calls us to be there for others who are in pain.

2. ENTER INTO THE FELLOWSHIP OF SUFFERING

> For just as the sufferings of Christ flow over into our lives, so also through Christ our comfort overflows. If we are distressed, it is for your comfort and salvation; if we are comforted, it is for your comfort, which produces in you patient endurance of the same sufferings we suffer. And our hope for you is firm, because we know that just as you share [literally, fellowship] in our sufferings, so also you share in our comfort. (2 Corinthians 1:5-7, NIV)

Early in our ordeal, a friend of a friend wrote to me, "There is a fraternity of suffering people. It's not an official group, and we haven't posed for a photo yet, but we know each other when we meet. Not one of us applied for membership. Suddenly we found ourselves having been inducted into this order."

No, none of us applied, but all were invited. We are not called to a pain-free life. In fact, Peter said,

> Do not be surprised at the painful trial you are suffering, as though something strange were happening to you. But rejoice that you participate [literally, fellowship] in the sufferings of Christ, so that you may be overjoyed when his glory is revealed. (1 Peter 4:12-13, NIV)

Paul actually celebrated entering into the fellowship of suffering, and he aspired to enter it more deeply.

> But whatever was to my profit I now consider loss for the sake of Christ. What is more, I consider everything a loss compared to the surpassing greatness of knowing Christ Jesus my Lord, for whose sake I have lost all things. I consider them rubbish, that I may gain Christ and be found in him, not

having a righteousness of my own that comes from the law, but that which is through faith in Christ—the righteousness that comes from God and is by faith. I want to know Christ and the power of his resurrection and *the fellowship of sharing in his sufferings*. (Philippians 3:7-10, NIV, emphasis added)

What does it mean to participate in the sufferings of Christ? I don't think it has anything to do with completing what Christ did on the cross. Jesus said, "It is finished" (John 19:30, NIV). I think it has everything to do with entering into the pain that the members of His body suffer today. Paul lived and breathed this. He entered into it with his whole being.

I fill up in my flesh what is still lacking in regard to Christ's afflictions, for the sake of his body, which is the church. (Colossians 1:24, NIV)

Besides everything else, I face daily the pressure of my concern for all the churches. Who is weak, and I do not feel weak? (2 Corinthians 11:28-29, NIV)

BREAKING THROUGH ISOLATION

We are invited into the deep bonds that form among those who suffer together. Calvin, my twenty-year-old son, is seriously considering joining a fishing crew off Kodiak Island in Alaska next summer. The owner, who recruits college students from all over the States, tells me that members of his crew generally become friends for life as they sometimes work twenty hours a day and occasionally risk their lives for one another. Christ wants us to experience that kind of bond with Him and with the members of His body.

Sometimes we are drafted into the fellowship of suffering when pain tragically breaks into our lives. At other times, we voluntarily participate when we choose to be there for others in pain.

People in pain often feel isolated and overwhelmed. They feel that no one really understands, that no one really bears the burden with them. To some degree, that's true. Proverbs 14:10 says that each heart knows its own bitterness, and no one else can fully enter into it. So don't say "I know how you feel" when you really don't and can't. That can feel like you're making light of that person's pain.

But people in pain also long for someone to genuinely enter in as much as possible, to draw near and carry the burden with them. Galatians 6:2 calls us to "carry each other's burdens, and in this way you will fulfill the law of Christ" (NIV). When we landed in the hospital with Ian, Renee's best friend said to her, "I will be here with you no matter what happens." And she kept her promise, for fifteen months and beyond to today. There were many nights when we would find ourselves alone with Ian, feeling overwhelmed and afraid, and she would show up just to be with us.

So where do you start? You might begin by simply saying from the heart, "I'm so sorry." If they sense that is coming from deep within you, they will find comfort in how you are drawing near and entering into their pain. You can say, "I can't fully understand what you are feeling, but I'm hurting with you." It may be less helpful to say, "I can't imagine what you are feeling." That tends to confirm their feelings of isolation.

Sometimes the best way to enter in is to say nothing and simply weep with those who weep. After Ian's memorial service, friends waited in line for hours to give us comfort. I remember little or nothing of what was said there. But I vividly remember one dear friend who, after waiting for so long, simply threw her arms around me and wept. She had nothing to say, yet she had everything to say. That touched me deeply. Maybe all you need to say is, "Can I give you a hug?" Physical comfort can sometimes say so much more than words.

YOUR STORY, OUR STORY

We can also enter into another person's pain by sharing our own stories. Paul went there as he continued to teach the Corinthians about suffering and comfort:

> We do not want you to be uninformed, brothers, about the hardships we suffered in the province of Asia. We were under great pressure, far beyond our ability to endure, so that we despaired even of life. Indeed, in our hearts we felt the sentence of death. But this happened that we might not rely on ourselves but on God, who raises the dead. (2 Corinthians 1:8-9, NIV)

In context, this is a remarkable confession. Much of 2 Corinthians is a response to Paul's critics. But here he makes himself vulnerable by sharing how he had gotten so depressed because of his own suffering that he sincerely wanted to die. Have you ever been brought that low through suffering? Paul felt it was important for the Corinthians to know he had been there. He opened his heart to them, hoping they would open their hearts to him.

The hazardous part of sharing your own story is that it may be more than the person in pain wants to hear or bear. Because we have lived our suffering in such a public way, sometimes folks assume that we want to enter into the suffering of others. They want to introduce us to others with cancer. We sometimes end up feeling like, "Don't ask me to enter into their pain when I can barely handle my own right now." We *have* entered into others' pain, though. Even now we closely follow the story of another family with a child near death. We exchange intimate notes and feelings with them that we share with few others. During our many weeks in the pediatric intensive care unit, we entered into the pain of a few others there, very few. You can only take on so much when you yourself are stripped bare by pain.

But in the right time and situation, it can be deeply comforting to be invited into the story of another even while you are living out your own story. It can be a welcome distraction. It can bring redemptive meaning to your own pain, wringing value out of it for others.

The fellowship of suffering is not an exclusive club. We're all invited. Some are drafted, although we can dodge the draft by choosing to live in isolation. But if you enter in, you will find it to be a place of deep bonds with Jesus and the members of His body.

3. BE THERE FOR OTHERS AS THE FATHER HAS BEEN THERE FOR YOU

> [God] comforts us in all our troubles, so that we can comfort those in any trouble with the comfort we ourselves have received from God. For just as the sufferings of Christ flow over into our lives, so also through Christ our comfort overflows. (2 Corinthians 1:4-5, NIV)

I don't know all of God's purposes for allowing pain into your life. But I know one: He intends to comfort you so that you will comfort others. In fact, He intends the comfort you receive from Him to be so abundant that it can't help but overfllow into the lives of others. Once you have entered into another person's pain, that comfort can take a lot of different practical forms—listening, talking, serving, or just showing up. But before we can comfort others in these ways, we have to get past the biggest obstacle the Devil puts in our way: self-centeredness.

When we are in pain, all of our natural instincts strain toward protecting and preserving ourselves. Some of that is God given. We do need to take care of ourselves, particularly when we are hurting. Pain is like the warning light that calls for attention. But sin tries to distort that and push us into destructive self-centeredness.

ANOTHER KIND OF CANCER

Rising above self-centeredness isn't easy for anyone, but it takes a special kind of courage for someone who is sick and facing a possible death sentence. In the thick of things, I prayed that Ian would find that courage. Three months into his cancer, I wrote this to friends:

April 26, 2008

> I'm praying that Ian will not only endure well, but that he'll rise above just surviving and reach out beyond himself to bless those around him. Cancer patients can get self-centered. After all, this is hard! But self-centeredness is a cancer of its own. I'm praying that in the midst of all this, Ian will find the courage to rise above self-centeredness to give and to bless and to love.

Ian did find the courage to get outside of himself. His courage inspired the Olympic athletes. He became an asset to the nurses in the oncology clinic, encouraging other patients to put their pain in perspective. He refused to cave in on himself emotionally. He lived every day to the fullest and dragged others along with him.

When Ian was diagnosed, his big sister Nicole Lorelei struggled with whether or not to move back east to attend school as she had planned. One day she was pushing Ian around the block in his wheelchair and began to mention her dilemma. Before she could finish the sentence, he said, "You need to go. I want you to go." In spite of her reservations, with his encouragement, she did go. The cancer of self-centeredness was being defeated so that Ian could be there for others.

AS LONG AS HE WANTS

Linda, too, learned how to fend off those moments of self-centered pity, which sneak up on us when we've most vulnerable. Near the end of a fourteen-month round of chemo, she was feeling worn out and weary of being the "fine example" of how to live through adversity. She wrote this to her church:

> People tell me I'm amazing, strong, full of faith, an inspiration. I want to put my fingers in my ears and scream. The truth is, I'm acting like a jerk.
>
> I lay in bed last night unable to sleep because everything hurt. Lying in bed wide awake but trying to sleep seems to be the best time to feel sorry for oneself, so I did. Blistered feet, stinging mouth, constant weariness, no physical energy, hair mostly gone, skin ravaged—the usual. Then I got mad at God because I'm just tired of this whole thing. Seven years is long enough. Haven't I learned whatever it is I'm supposed to have learned by now? Hasn't He used me to "inspire" enough people by now? Can I quit already? Use someone else to tell Your story, God!
>
> Then I remembered Stan's mother-in-law. Stan, a friend of my brother, is a Kenyan. His mother-in-law in Nairobi was recently diagnosed with cancer. It's not the best place to have cancer because the medical care she's receiving would be nowhere near what we have available here. Apparently, her family's not taking it well, so I sent a note of encouragement to her through Stan.
>
> It exploded. By that I mean it got passed along to other family and friends, and eventually I received word that it was being used in women's Bible studies in Kenya as proof of God's faithfulness and healing power. I don't even recall what I wrote; the real author was God. He just used my e-mail.
>
> Then I remembered Mary, a woman who lives in the hills of Kentucky. We met briefly a couple of months ago when she was

visiting her sister here and she came into my shop. Her eyes looked so lifeless, her demeanor forlorn. I was touched by how sad she seemed. When she stepped out of the room, her sister told me Mary has cancer and that she'd been given six months to live. Mary clearly had given up on life. You could tell that just from looking at her unsightly wig.

I talked to Mary awhile, told her about my own cancer, and somehow got her to laugh. She seemed to trust me and told me that her nails were peeling. Mine were also (a result of our drugs), and I offered to give her the nail strengthener I'd bought that morning. Coincidence? Hmm. She balked but finally took it with a smile, grateful for the special gift from a stranger.

Her sister returned to see me a couple of days later, saying Mary couldn't stop talking about our chance encounter. Mary had left school at thirteen, and, in her sister's words, "is a simple but sweet woman." Well, maybe she wasn't highly educated, but she had a heart that touched mine. Apparently she had little local support back home and was living this nightmare mostly alone. Mary was without hope, scared and discouraged, and crying every day. I got her address and wrote to her, telling her I'd continue to pray and that I hoped her nails were stronger.

A few days ago, I got a letter back. She'd gone home and bought a new wig! Praise God—not for the wig, but that she cares about herself again! She was feeling better, and she said she'd begun to pray for me, too. She said she's reminded that God does care for her, and she asked me to write again. She looks forward to something. Depressed people don't look forward to anything.

I wasn't even supposed to be in my shop that day. God put me there, and Mary too. It may seem that I encouraged Mary, but it's she who encouraged me. We seem to have nothing in common, except, oh yeah, we have cancer and know God. That's all it takes.

I won't list all the others who came to mind last night while I lay awake. I eventually fell asleep, but not before apologizing to God *for being a brat. If it weren't for the cancer, I'd have no knowledge of these people. My life is so much better than theirs, in terms of my care, my circumstances, my support system, my prognosis. Who am I to complain? God can use me to tell His story as long as He wants. Wait a minute! . . . Oh, never mind. As long as He wants.*

Oh, how I love my sister!

THE POWER OF SHOWING UP

Just as the Father of compassion is there for us, we're called to be there to comfort others in pain. One of the simplest ways to do that is to just show up. I once had a fellow on my leadership team who was bemoaning his lack of strategic contribution. But he, more than anyone else on our team, was shepherding our people. It's true that he rarely had a strategic plan, but I used to say that he had the "ministry of showing up." He just had a knack for being there when people most needed him.

Helping people in pain is not that complex. Yes, it can get complicated, but at the root, it's simply being there for them as God is there for us. We do not have to be heroic or extraordinary. Mother Teresa once said, "In this life we cannot do great things. But we can do small things with great love." Some of the greatest comfort I've received has been so simple. A friend would show up with tears in his eyes, pray briefly, then leave. And that was enough for that day. Renee's best friend would arrive with knitting in hand and sit and quietly pray. When Ian died, my college roommate dropped everything to fly across the country to be there with me. That was a priceless gift.

Others tried too hard to be profound or fix things. It seemed they were too uncomfortable with our pain to just sit with us in it. The most comforting friends have been those who don't need us to protect them from our pain.

There are also people who presume and invade our emotional boundaries without invitation or permission. It can be hard to know if you are one of the people who should be there for a friend in pain. In some cases, it will be obvious. In others, you might need to ask indirectly, through a subtle note or through a third party. Sometimes it's just a matter of timing. Since Ian died, several discerning friends have said to us, "Whenever you would like to talk about Ian, give me a call. I'd love to be with you at that time." That's wisdom that comes from walking the path of pain.

THE POWER OF LISTENING

When God does call you to be there for a friend in pain, your most important role is to be fully present and to listen, not to pry or to preach. Job's friends showed up. They sat with him and shared his agony for days. They were at their best when they were silent.

When they opened their mouths, they lost their redemptive influence. Although they had come to help, they had not come to listen. That became evident when Job poured out his heart to them. Although he did not curse God, he was not in a good frame of mind either, and his friends thought they needed to correct him. Job's situation frightened them. They thought if tragedy could hit Job, it could hit anyone. His pain made them feel vulnerable, so they tried to come up with possible explanations that would make them feel safe. When Job spilled out his agony, they found it difficult to just listen. I wonder what would have happened if they had just listened? Swiss physician and author Paul Tournier said that being listened to is so close to being loved that most people can't tell the difference. There are many times when people have come to me for counsel and left feeling encouraged because I simply listened. Sometimes they've even praised me for my wisdom when I actually said very little. Are you afraid you won't know what to say when you are with someone in pain? That's okay. "Even a fool is thought wise if he keeps silent, and discerning if he holds his tongue" (Proverbs 17:28, NIV).

Listening means not probing or trolling for information. "How are you?" can be a hazardous question for someone who is in pain. I sometimes dread that question and fend it off by saying, "Fine!" or "I'm doing far better than I deserve—but not nearly as well as God intended." That leaves them thinking. But "How are you?" can also be a welcome question when it comes at the right time from someone who has demonstrated sustained interest in us and is prepared to really listen. Then it becomes an opening for sincere listening rather than conversation filler or information gathering.

THE POWER OF LIFE-GIVING WORDS

There is great comfort in listening, but there is also a time to open our mouths and allow life-giving words to flow. Often those come in written form. Written notes have the advantage of giving us the freedom to receive and process them when we're ready. We love reading our CaringBridge guestbook. When Ian was at his worst, he would often refuse television or music but would nearly always enjoy having us read notes from friends.

There were times when the doctors' words would suck the life right out of us, drowning out the words the Father wanted us to hear. But then friends would come speak truth over us, renouncing fear and hopelessness with God's promises. These words breathed new life into us. Life-giving words can be gentle reminders to find joy. They can be tender nudges from those who have walked the same road. Life-giving words kindly share and build faith, and remind us of truth without preaching platitudes.

But beware of following Job's friends into trying to explain tragedy. Some of our friends felt like they needed to say something spiritual and wise after Ian died. The most common was "He's better off in heaven." That's so obvious, and somehow it felt like putting a Band-Aid on an amputation. They were saying what we already *knew* very well but did not *feel* right then. It was true, but not helpful.

Recently, Renee met someone in a church small group who had not known Ian but felt compelled to say something about his death. She said, "Maybe the Lord took Ian home because He knew that if he had lived longer, he would have fallen into a life of sin." That may be true, but there is no comfort for us in those words.

We have received notes from friends trying very hard to teach us what they thought we needed to know. There are times when that is needed, but it is usually from a close friend who has earned the privilege of serving as a guardrail when he or she sees that we are about to careen off into an emotional or theological ravine. But other notes were written by people who were just desperately trying to make sense out of what was happening to us. I think that is where Job's friends were.

Pain can push you to question what you think you know and believe. And sometimes we can allow it to push us beyond what the Scriptures say or teach. We desperately want to reconcile the goodness and power of God that we know with the horror and agony that we sometimes experience in this broken world. There is a technical name for that: *theodicy* (the vindication of God's goodness and providence in view of the existence of evil). I recently noticed that *theodicy* rhymes with *idiocy*. How ironic! From Genesis through Revelation, the Scriptures present both God's goodness and the evil of this world side by side without apology. We do well to do the same. Explanation is not what is needed most when we're in the midst of our pain.

In spite of all these cautions, don't be too afraid that you will say the wrong thing. Life-giving words overflow from love-filled hearts. Even if you say the wrong thing, if sincere love is your motive, the receiver will sense that. The apostle Peter was right when he said that "love covers a multitude of sins" (1 Peter 4:8, NASB). And long before that, wise King Solomon said, "Words kill, words give life; they're either poison or fruit—you choose" (Proverbs 18:21, MSG).

THE POWER OF LIFE-GIVING ACTIONS

Even life-giving words can't stand alone. If a picture is worth a thousand words, actions must be priceless. So the apostle John wrote, "Dear children, let us not love with words or tongue but with actions and in truth" (1 John 3:18, NIV).

For some people, like Renee, this comes naturally. Renee walks into a situation and knows just what to do to bring life-giving help. She finds joy in doing so. Others, like me, need to work at this. But we can learn—and the Holy Spirit is right there to help us. Remember the Holy Spirit is "the Comforter." You've experienced Him comforting you. You can also enjoy Him comforting *through* you. He's really good at this. Early this morning, He prompted me to write a note of encouragement to someone I hadn't seen or had any contact with in a couple of months. So at 6:15, I sent off an e-mail. Within an hour, I received a response marveling at how much she needed to hear just what I had shared. These actions don't come naturally to me, but when I listen to the Holy Spirit, I get to be in on His holy work of comforting others.

When people are in pain, they often don't really know what they need, which is another reason to be sensitive to the Spirit. "Let me know if there's anything I can do" is rarely helpful. Most will never call. They don't want to impose, or they can't think far enough in advance to make it convenient for you to help. Plus, it can feel humbling to be on the receiving end. What we've found most helpful is when others take practical initiative to do what they believe would be helpful.

After her baby died, our friend Leura summed it up well: Just do what you do. You know what you enjoy. You know how God uses you. You may be a house cleaner, a casserole maker, a flower sender, a child-care provider, or a letter writer. In our pain we want the huggers to hug, the pray-ers to pray, the givers to give, and the nurses to nurse. Spare us the awkwardness of trying to be something that you are not. It's okay. Just do what you do. Paul encouraged the church in Rome: "Let's just go ahead and be what we were made to be, without enviously or pridefully comparing ourselves with each other, or trying to be something we aren't" (Romans 12:6, MSG).

When you visit, you might bring some healthy snacks or even a meal. Rather than saying, "Let's get together sometime," just show up and ask, "Would this be a good time to go out for ice cream?" Or just bring the ice cream (our favorite comfort food) and be prepared to leave it if it's not a good time. Leave a note with money earmarked, "For something just for you." One friend got creative and went from restaurant to restaurant asking them to donate coupons or gift certificates for our family. That was practical and fun.

On several occasions, Linda's neighbor would bring over a pot of homemade soup and a large bowl of chocolate chip cookie dough, knowing how much Linda's husband enjoys the raw dough and Linda likes the baked cookies. That sweet, simple gift helped them endure their ongoing pain.

If you are close enough to the hurting person, you could offer to coordinate the help he or she needs. Pain is utterly exhausting. It can be overwhelming to make it through the day, much less think about what is needed for tomorrow. More than once, others coordinated healthy meals for us. At one point, when Ian needed 24/7 care at home, a friend coordinated volunteer caregivers and helpers through an online calendar. My co-workers sacrificially stepped in to lift my responsibilities or release me from obligations.

We usually celebrate and honor those who travel overseas to touch lives. But some of the most beautiful and powerful expressions of Christ's life flow very close to home: "The King will reply, 'I tell you the truth, whatever you did for one of the least of these brothers of mine, you did for me'" (Matthew 25:40, NIV).

4. PRAY AS IF IT'S THE MOST YOU CAN DO

> On him we have set our hope that he will continue to deliver
> us, as you help us by your prayers. Then many will give thanks
> on our behalf for the gracious favor granted us in answer to
> the prayers of many. (2 Corinthians 1:10-11, NIV)

"Has it come to that?" This is what one of my team members often
quips when we turn to prayer in our meetings. We laugh at how we
have droned on in our discussions without consciously and corporately
turning to our Leader. Then we get down to what may be the most
important part of our meeting: praying.

Isn't it strange how we think of prayer as the least we can do? How
often have you felt a pang of guilt as you said to a friend, "I'll pray for
you!" when you wish you could do more. It may be that you should
be doing more. But it also may be that praying is the most important
contribution you can make.

One of Linda's friends wrote this in response to Linda's request for
prayer: "This is grueling for you, to be sure. Oh, dear Linda, to pray
you through this is the most logical, sensible, and right thing to do, and
yet it does not relieve the immediate 'get me out of this!' sensation you
must go through constantly." Yet some of the most comforting words
we hear are "I'm really praying for you." We sense in our spirits when
someone means that, and it tells us that even when he or she is not with
us, that person is *with us* in a vital way. It matters. Love is conveyed in
praying. Soon after Ian fell into seizures, one of our pastors asked if he
could bring a woman to pray for Ian, a woman gifted in healing prayer.
She was a stranger to us, and we were reluctant until we heard that God
had already placed Ian so deeply on this woman's heart that she had
been praying and fasting for him for days. We've often said that if you
love our kids, we feel loved. We felt loved by this woman before we ever
met her. Sincere and earnest prayer is not the least we can do; it is one
of the most pivotal ways to enter into the fellowship of suffering.

One of the most precious experiences of our ordeal came one night through a global prayer meeting. People all over the world agreed to pray at a set hour. An intimate circle gathered around Ian's bed. But there were circles of friends fanned out around the globe. Several dozen youth gathered at our church and poured out their hearts for Ian. They paced the floor with open Bibles, crying out to God for Ian. Others prayed alone, but not alone. Many marveled at participating in a global gathering before the throne. I like to imagine that prayer meeting as front-page news in heaven that day.

Prayer is an opportunity to enter into the life of another in the most powerful and intimate way. People often asked Linda what they could do to help, offering meals, rides, and so forth. She always found their prayers to be the most effective help they could give, and she learned that admitting her own weakness—and acknowledging where true strength originated—was the surest way to be strong again:

> Ladies, I'd like some prayer, please. Yesterday afternoon I began to feel lousy, and by the time I closed the shop, I knew I was ill. I could barely close up, and it hurt to move. Steve wanted to take me out to dinner, but all I wanted to do was curl up under a blanket and not move. Turns out I had a fever. Those rascally little white cells are apparently still on vacation! Today I feel mostly fine, except for the "not wanting to move" part. I thought I'd pulled a muscle in my abdomen but wasn't really sure, what with all the other achiness. Well, today it's clear I did, and I'd like your prayers for strength, wickedly strong white cells, and all the rest. I have to be well enough for chemo in two days so it can knock me down again. Sigh. Thank God I have you who know Him, and thank God He is our source.

The following day Linda reported back:

> I don't know what you all said to God, but I felt great
> all afternoon! It was pretty amazing. The pulled muscle
> wasn't bothering me, and my temperature was normal. I
> had energy to last all day and even went out to dinner!
> Thanks for taking my request to God, and please thank
> Him for His answers. You know that Holy Spirit thing
> we've been studying? Well, He is alive and active among
> us. Now, to get through the chemo tomorrow morning. I
> can do this. My brother sent this to me from our late
> Dad's journal: "Jesus is not pushy. He just moves into
> the places that we vacate for Him."

PRAYING THE IMPOSSIBLE

We've written two chapters on prayer and talked about it throughout
this book. Yet we still can't convey how important prayer has been to
us as we've journeyed through our pain. Linda expressed it this way in
a letter to her friends:

June 15, 2009

> Last month's sermon on praying for "impossible" things was very
> meaningful to Steve and me. It shouted "Ian!" to our hearts. We
> prayed miracles for Ian for fifteen months, and no one who knew
> him will ever be the same. I can honestly say that not one person
> in the extended Lyons family will ever go back to our pre-Ian prayer
> lives. Through his dad's CaringBridge blog, thousands of people have
> been forever changed by the experience of praying for the impossible.
> At first we prayed with frightened, tenuous hope. Then we prayed
> with growing belief. Finally, despite our earnest prayers, Ian died.

But he left behind him people who know God better, love God more deeply, and trust God more completely. Rather than convincing us that praying for miracles is not worth the pain, it convinced us of God's power and love, and drew us closer to Him.

Yes, we did see miracles. We saw people who had never given God a second thought turn to Him in wondering prayer. We saw doubters recommit their lives to Jesus in faith. We saw teenagers turn to God in faith by praying for Ian, living out what they had learned as children but had never put into practice. We saw God choose specific times to show His power and mercy in the most unexpected ways. We were constantly surprised by the things He did for Ian and for the ways He continued to reveal Himself to the rest of us.

I met an interesting, likable young man at Ian's funeral. He knew Ian through the Olympic Training Center near the hospital, where he was a trainer. This young man has multiple piercings and tattoos and a "man of the world" demeanor. Still, I was drawn to him, because he clearly loved Ian. He told me that he had been confirmed in the church as a child but had walked away from it soon after, living the worldly life he wanted. He is a kind and loving man, but not yet clear on who God is or how He could possibly fit into his own life.

Yet he posted a note to Ian on the CaringBridge site that said, "Hey, Buddy! I just prayed for you. I don't know if I did it right, but at least I tried!" Can you imagine how that thrilled God!? He also told me that knowing Ian and our family had changed him forever, that he was taking a whole new look at the God of his youth, that God isn't who he'd thought He was. His last words to me that day were "I have a lot of thinking to do." He's been changed forever, and I don't doubt the angels will someday rejoice when he asks Jesus into his heart.

This is only one story; there are more. Miracles do happen, even if they're not always the ones we ask of God. Still, it's always worth it to ask for them. After all, God is better at choosing which ones are needed the most. Our desire for the miracle of life on earth for

Ian was not granted, but we still trust and believe in God, for Ian now lives in Him.

DON'T WASTE THE PAIN

I recently read a wonderful biography of Abraham Lincoln, and I am still marveling at the man.[2] Pain marked his life from beginning to end. Yet somehow he allowed his pain to make him greater and greater. Humble beginnings, lifelong ridicule of his sad face and gangly body, repeated failures and defeats all prepared him to lead our country through its most painful days.

Lincoln did not waste his pain. He allowed it to make him more—much more—than others around him. He gathered the strongest leaders of his day around him and rose above them because of his wisdom and compassion, qualities that had been forged in his pain. His steel resolve for noble purposes could not be broken by fear of pain. He had already been there and back.

He presided over some of the bloodiest carnage of war ever seen on earth, leaving almost 700,000 dead from their injuries. Nearly every family in the country was wounded by death. But Lincoln did more than merely preside; he waded into the pain around him. In spite of warnings about his own safety, he would often visit the battlefront. Tears would course down his cheeks as he walked among the dead and dying. And as he did, he grew. His soul grew so that he could shepherd his people through their darkest days. He loved them, and they knew it deep in their hearts.

We all have choices to make about how we respond to pain. Near the beginning of Lincoln's administration, his little son Will died. Mary Lincoln chose the way of greater pain as her response. It made her less rather than more. She lived in self-centered fear and misery. Her husband, on the other hand, allowed his pain to enlarge him for his destiny.

After years of living through a "curse" that has turned into a blessing, Linda now says this about Lincoln:

> I'm certainly no Lincoln, but God has also enabled me to use my own pain to become something more than I ever was before cancer invaded my life. Even I marvel at how easy it sometimes now seems to endure the ongoing disabilities I deal with daily—pain, heart problems, brain damage, physical weakness. None are easy! Still, I cannot recall a time of more true happiness or witness in my entire life. Though weaker in body, I feel stronger than I did ten years ago since I no longer walk by my own strength, but that of Jesus.

A few days ago I received a heart-wrenching note from a mother whose twelve-year-old son died from a brain tumor just a few weeks ago. My soul howled with agony. I careened through fresh memories of those first moments and hours and days and weeks following Ian's death. It is bitter to welcome a grieving mother into our fellowship of suffering.

In the fellowship of suffering, it is vital to reach outside of yourself to help others who are in pain. At *dontwastethepain.com* you can not only learn to grow through your pain, but you can also learn to help others. Join the fellowship, and continue to learn to *grow* through your suffering.

As I lay in bed, I wondered how to gently coax her out from under her pain, lest her pain shape her in destructive rather than redemptive ways. I half dreamed, half imagined a prisoner of war who refuses to be defined by his circumstances, a man whose soul has somehow grown larger than his cell, larger than his captors, larger than his pain. I dreamed of a man whose captors secretly stand in awe of him, wondering what kind of man could endure what he endures with such dignity, what kind of person could find joy and even sing in the night in spite of all the pain they inflict on him.

I long to be that kind of man in the face of my pain. I long for this mother to join us in the fellowship of sufferers who rise above their pain to become more. And we long for you to join us.

Where will your pain lead you?

QUESTIONS FOR REFLECTION

- ▶ Are you being called to "be there" for someone who is in pain? Who?
- ▶ How can you "just do what you do" to help that person?
- ▶ What do you hope will stick with you from this book?

NOTES

Chapter 3: OXYGEN
1. *The Abyss*, directed by James Cameron (Century City, CA: Twentieth Century-Fox, 1989).
2. "Live Jesus!" is David's life motto. He picked it up from Madame Jeanne de Chantal, a sixteenth-century French Catholic, one of the founders of the Sisters of Visitation.

Chapter 5: A THIN PLACE
1. Michael Mullen, "Croagh Patrick: A Perspective," http://www .thinplaces.net/michaelmullen.htm.
2. Randy Alcorn, *Safely Home* (Carol Stream, IL: Tyndale, 2003), 376.

Chapter 7: BUT THE PHYSICIANS
1. Ben Carson, *Think Big* (Grand Rapids, MI: Zondervan, 1992), 243.

Chapter 8: PRAYING IN THE FACE OF PAIN
1. Transcribed from Joni Eareckson Tada's message at Dallas Theological Seminary on "The Theology of Suffering."

Chapter 9: WHAT IF GOD SAYS NO?
1. Transcribed from Joni Eareckson Tada's message at Dallas Theological Seminary on "The Theology of Suffering."
2. James N. Bruce III, *From Grief to Glory: A Book of Comfort for Grieving Parents* (Carlisle, PA: The Banner of Truth Trust, 2008), 87, 89.

3. Bruce, 150.
4. Bruce, 159.
5. John Claypool, *Tracks of a Fellow Struggler: How to Handle Grief* (Waco, TX: Word Books, 1974), 67.

Chapter 10: WHEN WILL IT END?
1. Charles R. Swindoll, "Lessons from Suffering," January 12, 2005, http://www.dts.edu/media.
2. Viktor Frankl, *Man's Search for Meaning*, 3rd ed. (New York: Simon & Schuster, 1984), 80–81.
3. Oswald Chambers, *My Utmost for His Highest* (New York: Dodd Mead & Co, 1935), September 30 entry.
4. Chambers.

Chapter 11: GOT JOY?
1. Nancy Guthrie, *The One Year Book of Hope* (Carol Stream, IL: Tyndale, 2005), 269.
2. Jerry Sittser, *A Grace Disguised* (Grand Rapids, MI: Zondervan, 1995), 50.
3. Kahlil Gibran, "The Prophet," http://www.math.miami.edu/~jason/gibran/kahlil/prophet_ch7.html.
4. Sittser, 49.
5. Encyclopedia.com, "Henry of Mondeville," http://www.encyclopedia.com/doc/1G2-2830901940.html.
6. Wikipedia, "Norman Cousins," http://en.wikipedia.org/wiki/Norman_Cousins.
7. Guthrie, 270.
8. Guthrie, 266.

Chapter 12: THE FELLOWSHIP OF SUFFERING
1. Nicholas Wolterstorff, *Lament for a Son* (Grand Rapids, MI: Eerdmans, 1987), 81.
2. Doris Kearns Goodwin, *Team of Rivals: The Political Genius of Abraham Lincoln* (New York: Simon & Schuster, 2005).

SCRIPTURE INDEX

About
the Authors

DAVID LYONS is an international vice president of The Navigators. He oversees international initiatives, communications, and networking of their five thousand staff in more than one hundred countries. David loves photography and hiking in the mountains of Colorado. David and Renee are the parents of seven children. Even with so many children, they often have friends live with them and frequently have guests around their table laughing loudly or quietly discussing their questions about life.

David's personal experience with Internet ministry led him to envision helping others to grow through their pain through this book, and through *www.dontwastethepain.com*. Come visit the website to see how God is bringing beauty out of ashes.

LINDA RICHARDSON is a former merchandise-display artist and garden gift-shop owner, now retired. She often works in her own quarter-acre garden when she is able. Other favorite pastimes include hiking the waterside peninsula where she lives with her husband, lying in her hammock, cooking, writing, and reading whatever she can find. She has two children, one in grad school and one in college. Living with cancer is a day-to-day adventure that she puts on the back burner when she can, while simply enjoying the rest of her life.